# The
# GREEN BABY

# The
# GREEN
# BABY

## 50 Practical Tips

### JOSEPHINE F. THOMAS

PB ISBN: 9781838060213
EBOOK ISBN: 9781838060206

British Library Cataloguing in Publication Data.
A catalogue record for this book is available from the British Library.

Typeset in the United Kingdom by Indie-Go
https://www.indie-go.co.uk

*This book is dedicated to all the women who had to give birth without their birthing partners during the coronavirus crisis, all the frontline health care workers and volunteers, and to those who became the victims of COVID-19 as well as their loved ones left behind.*

# CONTENTS

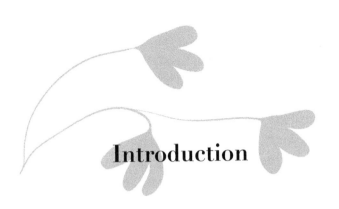

# Introduction

## Inception

The idea for this book came to me on a bright April morning when my daughter was only eight weeks old. She was still fast asleep after a short crying spell. To a baby's mind – and notably a newborn baby's – there is no such thing as the concept of time. Her crying meant this: *I. Want. Fed. Now!* So, it had all been down to me, still drowsy from sleep, to make some decidedly un-dexterous attempts to let her latch on and make myself comfortable (although by that time we had become rather proficient at breastfeeding and I had learnt to feed her lying down on my side). And yet, even thirty seconds seems far too long for a hungry baby. All done, I could lean back and watch her go back to sleep while listening to a whole orchestral performance of birdsong. That day, the swallows and house martins had made their first appearance after the long and dark winter months, which seem to last forever up here in Scotland. And then a bumblebee came to investigate the remains of last year's swallows' nest. I was tired too, but I couldn't go back to sleep and, just like the warm sun, my ideas began to flow.

I had always wanted my child to grow up in a place where she (or he) would have the chance to experience the natural world first-hand. For some time, I had believed it would never happen. Despite a lack of any experience in that regard, I was pretty sure I knew what I wanted for my child and how I would want to bring her up. Equipped with a mind conscious of environmental issues, it all seemed pretty straightforward. I read several books and browsed through quick clicks of the internet to assuage my anxiety, which began to revisit me every so often, and more frequently the closer I got to my due date and beyond. The world around us and our peers seemed to suggest that we needed a whole lot of 'things' to make it work. I sometimes felt stuck, lost in a labyrinth of must-haves, interfering (albeit well-meant) suggestions, and aggressive advertising of 'can't-do-withouts'.

And then my baby was here, and I stumbled into the wondrous world of motherhood. To my mind, it is the one of greatest joys you will ever experience in your life, and yet, it is also highly stressful, exhausting and confusing. Because of this, I wanted to create a little map or a guidebook. I hope you will find it helpful as you take your first cautious steps as a new parent. You probably did a lot of research, shopping and talking while you were pregnant. I mainly had mums and their babies in mind as I was writing this book, but I have also thought about all the others involved in this truly marvellous and life-changing experience. So, dads, grannies, grandads, uncles and aunts, come and join in.

The following list of questions was compiled throughout my daughter's first year of life while I followed her through her first attempts at rolling over, sitting up, bottom-shuffling, teething, crawling, babbling and first steps (and so much more). With hindsight, I revised and rewrote it after my baby had undergone a life-altering metamorphosis. In front of me stood and ran a rambunctious toddler, brimming with energy, inquisitiveness, cheekiness and love, and becoming ever more aware of being her own person. But that is another chapter. I have based all of my writing on personal observation, trial and error, and as much valuable and eye-opening research as I could get my hands and eyes on. Long before that (about halfway through my pregnancy), I had decided to start writing a blog.[1] I found this particularly helpful as it kept me focused and became an outlet (and inlet) for thoughts and issues very close to my heart. A lot of things about parenting seem to elude us, and just as you are trying to get it right the chance to do so often passes. I also believe that we cannot achieve true happiness through endless distraction in front of screens and consuming material goods, but through leading a simpler life and concentrating on what is meaningful (I don't mean important either, because a lot of things can be extremely meaningful without actually being important). We can't find simplicity and true contentment if we're always trying to outdo each other and compete against each other.[2]

It was when I found myself confused and exhausted after spending hours on end looking for the right equipment on websites that the idea to write this book took shape. While sufficient and appropriate clothing and the right food are essential for your baby, I doubt that you could not survive without a pram or a carrycot or

---

1   https://littlegreenfootpath.com
2   For a different take on fierce competition and its adverse effects on the human psyche, read Charles Eisenstein's *The Ascent of Humanity* (2013).

an expensive cot in a nursery with a matching wardrobe and chest of drawers. I have never once used a pram or a carrycot – I always carried my baby in a sling, and only used a pushchair later when she was getting quite heavy. We decided to purchase a so-called Next2Me cot, but once again, it didn't get used overly much. I do appreciate the advice against it, but I am now much in favour of co-sleeping/bedsharing. It has made things a lot easier for my baby, me, and my husband too, by the way. There is a lot to be said about this practice; I refer you to Tip 4.

## What this book is – and what it is not

This book focuses on the quite basic (but by no means simple) needs of newborns and babies before they reach the toddler stage (i.e. their first year of life); although anyone who has ever had a baby (and, not surprisingly, there are a lot of us) knows how huge a person already inhabits that tiny little body.

This book is not meant to tell you what you should or shouldn't do, nor is it based on years of medical expertise and experience. It is more likely to be read as a guide to responsive parenting[3], coupled with ideas for an environmentally conscious lifestyle without giving up some of the amenities we are so used to these days.

---

3   Responsive parenting or sensitive parenting refers to a parenting style in which parents are aware of their children's emotional and physical needs and respond accordingly. One of the key principles is unconditional love, i. e. not using the giving or withholding of affection as a form of reward and punishment. Further reading and information can be found here: https://www.physicianscenter.org/parents/parenting-resources/articles/sensitive-or-responsive-parenting/; https://www.goodtherapy.org/blog/7-principles-for-responsive-parenting-0715144.

You won't find any thoughts on strict routines such as those that have been promoted by Gina Ford;[4] nor do I advocate a completely anti-authoritarian upbringing or offer any medical advice. Mainly, I aim to share my thoughts on how we can begin to instil a sense of wonder in our children and help them to realise that, without the natural world in which we live, there is no life.

As part of my research, I have also interviewed a few professionals and friends who are experts in their respective fields. Their valuable and knowledgeable contributions can be found under the title *Ask the expert*.

## Who has all the answers?

Along the way, I asked myself some questions that you might have thought about, too:

- How can we protect our children from the incessant onslaught of technology on their senses and the feeling of alienation it engenders, without banning it from their lives entirely?
- How can we achieve a healthy balance? Are we still able to function if our electronic devices fail to do so?
- How can we build a future for our children in which wildflower meadows still exist, and in which there is still natural food which is unprocessed and actually looks like a piece of fruit or a vegetable?
- How can this more natural lifestyle lead to

4     https://www.telegraph.co.uk/women/womens-health/9126065/
This-time-Gina-Fords-taken-it-too-far.html

healthier children and families right from the start, even before they can walk?

- How can we avoid the trap of marketing ploys such as toys and clothing being separated according to two genders?
- What materials can we use instead of plastics (for shopping, personal care, toys – you name it)?
- How can we reduce the toxins in our homes and save a lot of money in the process?
- Where do we need to look for suitable toys and early learning materials for our babies? Have they been produced ethically and sustainably and are they safe to play with?
- How can we find out about ways to consume goods in an ethical, sustainable and healthy way?
- Which equipment is essential? Can we get by without some of these things? Are there other ways to get what we need without spending all of our savings?
- What is the best way to feed our babies?

The aim of this book is to help you see through a lot of the pitfalls that early parenthood entails. The suggestions are there for you to try out and to be adjusted according to your and your baby's specific needs.

# The GREEN BASICS

Going green with your baby is not just about what things to acquire. It is about how to get by on a limited budget; upcycling things without looking threadbare. Because you don't have to. In this sense, every letter of GREEN BASICS stands for one of the core aspects which build the groundwork for transformation of our daily lives. Overall, it is about making informed and ethical, as well as politically sound, lifestyle choices, while thinking about saving energy and buying local produce, reducing the use of fungicides and pesticides, and using your body to get about more in order to reduce carbon emissions.

## G: Generosity and Gratitude

*Do you feel you are part of a generous and reliable community? Do you think you can ask your neighbours for help? Do you know your neighbourhood?*

It seems that we are waking up to the fact that living in communities and establishing trust is essential for a healthy and happy life. Environmental biologists are now increasingly in favour of seeing the symbiotic coexistence of organisms as a selective advantage.[5] The fittest according to the updated theory are those who know how to help others and therefore themselves. But there is a lot to be said about reminding yourself of what we are taking for granted, and focusing on the simple and yet important things in life. This practice certainly helps when you are feeling frazzled (which you are bound to be), and it is also about sharing the load and accepting help.

# R: Recyclable

*How much do you recycle? What do you know about your local council's recycling scheme? Are you trying to upcycle as much as you can? Do you eat lots of fast food and ready meals, which are not only bad for your mind and body, but also produce a lot of packaging waste?*

Recycling is not just about dumping things in the right bin, which in itself is often somewhat of a challenge, especially when a product contains two or more materials. Packaging made of a mix of cardboard and plastic are a classic example. These are used to showcase toys or food. Another big problem is carry-out coffee cups.[6]

So, try and think about what you are using in your home. Upcycle old tea towels and use them as cleaning cloths; use old glass jars for storage[7] instead of buying plastic storage boxes, and for making home-made jams and preserves, or put tea lights in them.

---

5    https://www.ncbi.nlm.nih.gov/pmc/articles/PMC1317043/
6    https://littlegreenfootpath.com/2018/01/08/coffee-cups-and-waste-reduction/
7    For more tips on how to do this see my blog: https://littlegreenfootpath.com

# E: Ecological

*Do you know which labels to look out for when buying food and other consumer goods? Which products do you need to avoid?*

A lot of things style themselves as 'eco' and, as an umbrella term, it seems a little overcrowded and doesn't automatically mean a product is good for the environment. So simply buying something with that label won't make you eco-conscious; it is more about observing, trying things for yourself and reminding yourself of what you need, which very often isn't as much as you might think. You may want to try apps like Buycott[8] to help you with your consumer choices.

# E: Ethical

*Do you know who makes your clothes? Have you ever asked yourself how it is possible that some imported goods are so ridiculously cheap? How do you feel about veganism and a more ethical approach to food production and consumption?*

Globalisation has taken the exploitation of workers and resources to new heights. Modern slavery is a big problem, and we can't just avert our eyes and pretend it was only an issue in the distant past when people used to do things differently. As a consumer, you can choose products that benefit people, animals and the environment and will minimise the negative impact of our consumerist culture.[9]

8    https://www.buycott.com
9    See http://www.fairtrade.org.uk/, https://www.

Any physical product that needs to be transported in lorries and post vans or is stored in warehouses causes *some* environmental damage; it's more a question of whether other factors contribute to that damage further. Consider who makes them, and what is in them. Make that little extra effort by consuming less. You might want to have a look at the Ethical Trading Initiative (ETI),[10] an alliance of companies, non-governmental bodies and trade union organisations tackling issues like unequal supply chains and wages as well as modern slavery. You can also subscribe to Ethical Consumer[11] to find out about greener options for everyday items we use in our homes.

To discuss vegetarianism and veganism in their vast scope and all their implications would require me to write another book at least and would also exceed my own expertise at present. Vegetarianism and especially Veganism have become political statements and lifestyle choices, standing up for a compassionate and ethical treatment of animals and a more ethical and ecological economy.[12] Taking the pledge (and plunge) to go vegetarian or vegan is about a lot more than "just" cutting out meat and other animal produce such as eggs and dairy in your diet. It also means that you will need to look out for any ingredients in processed foods such as gelatine which are commonly added to deserts and sweets to thicken them.[13] Gelatine

---

crueltyfreeinternational.org/, https://www.ethicalconsumer.org/palm-oil-free-list and many more.

10   https://www.ethicaltrade.org/

11   https://www.ethicalconsumer.org/

12   https://www.theguardian.com/lifeandstyle/2018/apr/01/vegans-are-coming-millennials-health-climate-change-animal-welfare

13   https://www.thespruceeats.com/what-is-gelatin-1328467

is also a common ingredient in vitamin supplements, but manufacturers such as Vitabiotics are adding vegan options to their range.[14] Apart from food, most vegans would not wear leather shoes or wear any clothing made from animal-derived fibres. I will touch on some of the options in this book and provide references to some relevant websites if you are interested in obtaining more information about bringing up vegetarian/vegan babies or alternatives to Omega-3 fish oils in supplements or leather-free shoe wear. To find out more and get inspired visit sites such as Bohemian Hippy[15] and The Vegan Society.[16]

# N: Nutritious and Non-Toxic

*Are you sure that what you and your family are eating is healthy and nutritious? Do you know what ingredients are in your personal care products, and which can potentially put your health at risk?*

A lot of the least nutritious foods contain ingredients which are perhaps not exactly toxic, but bad for your health nonetheless. The first way to protect your family against these is to make your food from scratch. There are straightforward ways to do this. Support local and organic produce, and try to achieve a balance between imported and domestic produce in your diet.

---

14   https://www.vitabiotics.com/collections/vegan-ve
      getarian?gclid=EAIaIQobChMI4dSSxdD25gI
      VF-DtCh3F0gUMEAAYASAAEgKGA_D_BwE
15   https://www.bohemianhippy.com/
16   https://www.vegansociety.com/

# B: Biodegradable

*What kinds of disposable household items do you use?*
*What kind of household cleaning products do you use?*
*Have you considered using reusable nappies to cut down on*
*household plastic waste? Have you thought of any other ways*
*to minimise plastic waste? Do you have a compost bin?*

Use products with fewer chemicals in them. By switching to more eco-friendly cleaners, you will make your home a safer place not only for the environment, but also for yourself, your baby and the whole family. Using reusable nappies and choosing a brand of eco nappies instead of Pampers will also make a huge difference (see chapter 3). Look into the different types of plastics we use in our household and try and buy bin liners made from recycled plastic. Stop using freezer bags (use glass jars, reusable containers or paper bags) and ditch the cling film and kitchen foil. Leftovers can be put into a Pyrex bowl with a plate on top and stay nicely fresh in the fridge that way. Fruit can survive in sealable containers (plastic is probably OK in this case, as long as it is not single-use, but consider switching to stainless steel boxes[17]).

# A: Affordable

*How much money do you spend on things you are just*
*going to use once and then throw away? How long are toys*
*and clothes designed to last?*

You might be surprised to learn that going green will almost certainly save you a lot of money. You will sometimes need

---

17    https://elephantbox.co.uk/

to make an upfront investment, as with cloth nappies and organic mattresses and covers. But ultimately these are more economical as they are made to last and are more versatile. It's also good to swap items within a community and help each other. Another way to reduce costs is to learn to make things yourself without having to be an expert; or reduce your use of plastics by seeking out specific retailers and shops, and especially cutting down on single-use plastics or avoiding them altogether. There are vibrant online communities you can join to support your efforts. A lot of the tips in this book are about trying to find ways to enter parenthood on a budget. The first thing is to buy fewer items in the first place and to make use of charity shops and the Facebook market place. Another thing is to see if you can make things yourself or if they can be fixed. You could try sewing, for example. Work with what you have already got before you buy things. See if an old cupboard can be used for your baby's clothes or a chest of drawers can be used to store nappies. Wicker baskets that are hanging about in the loft will do to store baby's toys and books.

When it comes to food, you can also save a lot of money by cutting out ready meals and ordering them in. Plan the family menu a week ahead instead and only shop for what you need. Treats are important, but they should be seen for what they are: treats! Also be selective in what kind of toiletries you buy (see chapter 5). Go DIY with a lot of other things in your household, such as making your own cleaning agents (see chapter 6). And last but not least, stay away from electric gadgets like wet wipe warmers or electric baby rockers. You have got a pair of arms and a body to rock your baby and warm water from the tap to wet a flannel to wipe your baby's bottom! Going minimalist also means you will accumulate a lot less clutter which you will need to get rid of afterwards. It is another unnecessary stressor of modern life. We simply have too much of everything, so perhaps we should all try and hold ourselves back from starting our children's lives with too much clutter.

# S: Sustainable

*On a global scale, how many harvests do we have left before soil degradation progresses at an alarming speed? What do you think is your place in these times? Do you want to make changes to your consumer habits? Do you want to join an environmental working group or other organisation? Do you want to seek out more information to transform the way we live our lives to help preserve the planet that sustains us for future generations?*

Sustainability is about not extracting more than we can put back in. Try to find out whether the products you use are sustainably sourced or produced. Using sustainable products is important not only when it comes to the food we eat; it also includes the products we use in our bathroom. A lot of the time, they contain palm oil, which, along with soya beans[18] and cotton,[19] is one of the most devastating crops grown today. It is also worth thinking about the impact plants have on our environment in terms of food

---

18   https://www.theguardian.com/environment/2009/jun/21/ethical-living-soya

19   https://www.organiccotton.org/oc/Cotton-general/Impact-of-cotton/Risk-of-cotton-farming.php

miles; that is, if they have been flown halfway around the world from Argentina, Peru, Kenya or elsewhere. Do you need to eat strawberries in January? Asparagus in November? Parsnips in April? Going seasonal as well as local is another great way to help reduce food miles and the use of pesticides and fertilisers.[20]

# I: Informed

*Are you making use of all the resources available to you? Do you feel you have all the information necessary to make confident choices for yourself and your baby?*

Going green is also about knowing the options which are available to you, and that you can always opt out. Staying informed is essential in terms of, for example, public vaccination schemes, or communal and political decision-making processes. Short-term solutions driven by a competitive economy are causing utter devastation to our ecosystems and ultimately ourselves.

# C: Conscious

*Do you know of any forest schools in your area? Are you aware of any voluntary or communal work to protect the local environment? How do you want to raise this kind of awareness in your child?*

Be aware of what is going on around you. Raise awareness of environmental issues and the natural world, and lay the

---

20  https://www.vegsoc.org/cookery-school/blog/seasonal-uk-grown-produce/

foundations of a lifelong interest in your child. Do this without trying to teach anything specific. Exploration is the key at this stage, without having a particular goal in mind all the time.

# S: Social

*Do you know about ways to share your green efforts? Do you know where to look for guidance or more ideas?*

Share experiences and items with your community. Pass things on. Find out about smallholdings and allotments if you don't have enough garden space yourself, and connect with groups of like-minded people. Very often, another idea will come your way, and possibilities for new projects present themselves along with support.

# A word on pregnancy

Although this book does not include an in-depth discussion of the life-changing months of pregnancy, a lot of the decisions you make in that period will directly affect the relationship you'll have with your baby, so a few words on how you can already start being "green" before your baby has arrived should be made. The time your baby spends in the womb are crucial in establishing a bond between the baby, yourself and other family members. It includes the physical side of things such as the food you eat and the exercise you do, the supplements you choose to take as well as how much time you allow yourself to relax.

Reading is another important thing which you will find will still be easier to fit in than it will be in the months that follow the birth. Here are a few recommendations I found extremely helpful to accompany me on my journey.

## Grantly Dick-Read, Childbirth Without Fear (2013)

This book has a bit of an old-fashioned feel to it (the 1st edition is from 1944 and Dr Dick-Read attended to the wounded in the Gallipoli campaign in 1915). And yet, it is still current as the vanguard of the natural birth movement away from too much intervention. Dick-Read's ideas were revolutionary in focusing on the strength and the ability of the female body to do the birthing by itself, if allowed to be in the right frame of mind and basically act instinctively like a mammal. It is definitely worth a read.

### Ina May Gaskin, Ina May's Guide to Childbirth (2008)

This book is especially relevant for the American situation, where people travel across state boundaries to give birth on her farm. You are likely to end up enraged by what women had to endure (including the author herself) in the name of medical progress gone too far, including legs fastened in stir-ups, having no recollection of the birthing process due to anaesthetics and being denied any close contact with their newborn for sometimes as long as 24 hours, occasionally even longer. Read it to make you feel strong and empowered.

### Michel Odent, Birth and Breastfeeding (2003)

Another one of the early revolutionaries. He even claims men should again be banned from the birthing theatre altogether, as their presence is partly responsible for slowing down the process. It all sounds a bit quirky, but it is definitely worth a read. He is also a fervent supporter of prolonged breastfeeding and warns against the nutritional risks, both short and long-term of not nursing.

### Pam England, Ancient Map for Modern Birth: Preparation, Passage, and Personal Growth during your Childbearing Years (2017)

I read this only a week or two before I went into labour. Creative and intuitive, it will help you touch base with a less cerebral side of yourself and approach this life-changing event from a more spiritual and artistic side. It includes drawing and mind-mapping exercises to regain trust in your own authority.

Use the time preceding the big event, to reflect on yourself and your life up to this point and daydream about what lies ahead. There won't be a lot of downtime to do this once the baby has arrived. What kind of parent you would like to be? What do you wish for? Even get in touch with your fears. In my view, it is a lot more important to ask yourself some of these questions than to buy stuff. Seriously think about what breastfeeding means to you and where you stand with it in relation to your partner and your wider circle of relations and friends. Will they support your decision whatever it may be?

Exercise is not only important for your general health both during pregnancy and after delivery, but also to ensure that your baby is in the right position for birth. Swimming is an excellent exercise to achieve this, as is yoga. However, it makes sense to talk to your midwife or doctor before you decide on any exercise regimen. My midwife advised me to spend time on all fours as they used to in the old days when scrubbing tiled kitchen floors. The baby will then be able to move more freely, and perhaps another way of reminding us of our quadruped past. The way we are likely to sit these days leaning back in comfy chairs, the baby often gets lodged in our pelvis and doesn't have room to turn in time or lies in the womb like in a hammock. If you are experiencing difficulties, the "Spinning babies" website is a good resource.[21] Make sure you go to your antenatal classes and most of all the breastfeeding classes on offer. See if you can find a La Leche league group in your area.[22]

For your hospital bag get biodegradable nappies or even reusable ones[23], non-scented shampoos or soaps[24], and Natracare organic maternity pads[25] to deal with the lochia. For more information on birthing preparation I can only recommend booking yourself on a Hypnobirthing course.[26] These courses also contain a lot of advice on how to prevent tearing (use a Perineum massage oil[27], it helped me enormously) and most of all: write a birth plan. It will help you to feel more in control of your options which is a great step forward and is what Hypnobirthing is mostly about. It will also help the midwife on duty to work with you according to your wishes when the time comes.

And last but not least, stay away from toxic environments, both in body and mind.

---

21   https://spinningbabies.com/

22   https://www.laleche.org.uk/find-lll-support-group/

23   Read all about nappies in chapter 3.

24   More information about additive-free and safe cosmetics in chapter 5.

25   https://www.natracare.com/products/maternity/; for reusable nursing pads see chapter 1.

26   There are different associations which offer courses. I can only speak for Katharine Graves "Hypnobirthing" as it is the one I did, but do shop around and see if you feel more comfortable with one of the other ones available. Here is a list of useful sites: https://www.kghypnobirthing.com/; https://thepositivebirthcompany.co.uk/; http://www.thehypnobirthingassociation.com/

27   https://www.weleda.co.uk/perineum-massage-oil-50ml-606161

# Medical disclaimer

This book contains advice on green and healthy living which to my mind go hand in hand. I am not trained in the medical profession or naturopathy, although it is one of my great passions. The tips and advice you read here are based on my personal experience. I would therefore want to advise you, if you experience any adverse reactions with any of the natural remedies or recipes mentioned here, stop its use or application and seek medical assistance if symptoms persist. None of the advice here can be a replacement for a thorough consultation with one of your health professionals. When your baby, yourself or another family member are ill, seek professional advice. If any of the symptoms do not improve after a few days or you suspect an underlying condition, see your midwife or doctor. The author cannot be held responsible for the content of any of the websites which may have been altered subsequently.

# Feeding and Sleeping

*The newborn baby will only have three demands. They are warmth in the arms of its mother, food from her breasts, and security in the knowledge of her presence. Breastfeeding satisfies all three.*

Grantly Dick-Read, *Childbirth Without Fear*

Breastfeeding lies right at the very core of the mammalian mother-and-child relationship. It is where our evolutionary past resonates most strongly within us and is visible right in front of our eyes. It offers closeness, comfort, nutrition and nurture. Over the first few months of your baby's life, everything revolves around the two essential functions of feeding and sleeping (for you too, by the way). These are what newborn babies do most of the time, although, when you find yourself staggering about the house, bleary-eyed and still feeling bruised during those special six weeks after the birth, the so-called puerperium, it sometimes feels as though your baby isn't sleeping at all.

Once all the confusion and novelty has worn off,

however, something resembling a rhythm is very likely to emerge. By this, I mean a more responsive parenting approach which, unlike Gina Ford's routines,[28] you will need to work out individually to meet both your and your baby's needs. Breastfeeding and co-sleeping are essential as part of this parenting style, as they enable you to satisfy your baby's emotional need to be close to you along with providing optimal nourishment. In fact, in many societies, people would be astonished that we can even contemplate weaning our babies so early (which would be any time under the age of two years), or letting them sleep by themselves, let alone in a separate room.[29]

So why do we find ourselves in this predicament, whereby there is no scarcity of food and a reduced necessity for hard manual labour, and yet so often our bodies seem to fail us?

# TIP 1
## Breastfeed

*Breastfeeding comes first (it actually does; straight after birth), and why you should do it (your baby knows they want to go for the free vanilla milkshake)*

### Scenario 1

Grandmother/Mother: Oh, is she feeding *that* much? Perhaps she needs a bottle. *(Theatrical cue: make it sound*

---

28  https://www.theguardian.com/lifeandstyle/2003/jan/29/
    familyandrelationships.healthandwellbeing

29  https://www.naturalchild.org/articles/james_mckenna/
    cosleeping_world.html

*full of disbelief, and give the semblance of raking through some hazy memory of events which took place sometime in the 1980s or 1990s.)*

Mother/Daughter: No, Mum! *(Theatrical cue: sounding sleep-deprived, edgy and a little exasperated).*

Grandmother/Mother: But if she is hungry... *(Theatrical cue: sounding fretful and stiff. Subtext: I am only trying to help.)*

Mother/Daughter: Mum! I. Am. Not. Going. To. Give. Her. A. Bottle! *(No theatrical cue or subtext required.)*


## Scenario 2

Step-grandmother/Stepmother: Why does she want to feed again? There can't be that much in there. *(Theatrical cue: pointing at breasts with a raised eyebrow and a customary listen-to-me-I know-best-how-things-are-done attitude.)*

Mother/Stepdaughter: *Start explaining why it is important to build up a sufficient supply of milk this way (see Tip 2 in this book). Try not to be dismayed by the dismissive reply: "Oh, I see – interesting what they tell you these days", at which point your conversational partner swivels round and moves on to something else which is deemed more worth their while.*


Are you still with me? How nerve-racking can scenes like this be, particularly for young mothers? I am sure a lot of us are no stranger to similar situations. Everybody around us seems to know better and is trying to tell us how to get things right. The reasons why these comments left me relatively unfazed are deeply ingrained in my own life story (and the narrative I chose to tell and retell myself in order to come to terms with it), and it took long years of deep digging, disappointments, resilience and external help, such as professional counselling and the support of real friends and a loving partner, to get there. But what if you are more dependent on your parents' or other people's opinions? What if you care more about what they think?

Amy Brown has argued convincingly that none of these things will tell you directly not to breastfeed but it does mean that your baby is not being responded to and fed according to their needs. A bottle is given, a feed delayed, and a drop in milk supply is the consequence, through no fault of the mother herself. The problem is that she is ultimately made to feel that she is the one to blame, that her body has failed her. This is only going to add to the negative body image a lot of women have already.[30]

Gabrielle Palmer[31] made it very clear in her book "The Politics of Breastfeeding" that messages about the "benefits" of breastfeeding are misleading in that they give the impression of artificial feeding being the norm. We tend to do what is modelled and what other people around us do, so if hardly anybody we know breastfeeds for any length of time it is unlikely that it would be something we ourselves end up doing. Most of this is due to the way our society is organised, where pressures of working outside the home, shift work and public opinions dictate a mother's behaviour, very often by necessity, when not going back to work soon after birth may be unaffordable.[32]

---

30  Read Chapter 4 in Amy Brown's *Breastfeeding Uncovered* (2016) to learn more (see the Recommended Reading section of this book).

31  *The Politics of Breastfeeding*, Chapter 5, loc. 1017.

32  For a critical discussion on this, refer to https://www.theguardian.

As this book does not focus solely on breastfeeding, I won't be able to cover its complexities as thoroughly as I would like. Other people, amongst them Gabrielle Palmer and Dr Amy Brown, have done that before me and have done such a brilliant job, based on many years of research and experience, that there is no requirement. Nonetheless, as part of a more eco-conscious approach to parenting, breastfeeding comes first.

## Why do we struggle with breastfeeding?

On the face of it, we shouldn't. Next to procreating our species by engaging in sexual intercourse, which is the initial step in the egg-meets-sperm scenario, subsequently growing the baby inside our womb as *placentalia* naturally do, and then giving birth, feeding our young with our lactating breasts is the most straightforward way to bring them up and ensure the healthy continuation of the species. But why, then, does breastfeeding seem to be near enough impossible for so many of us? There may be reasons why, with the best of intentions, you won't be able to breastfeed for as long as you would like, maybe because financial pressures require you go back to work or because there are physical or mental illnesses such as PND (see Tip 48), and in some of these cases you will have to take a look into formula, which should then preferably be organic.[33]

---

com/commentisfree/2016/feb/02/my-mommy-tax-six-months-of-nursing-cost-more-than-a-year-of-formula and https://www.theguardian.com/science/brain-flapping/2015/mar/18/breastfeeding-raises-iq-worrying-questions

33  Another issue is supplementation with so-called LCPs (long-chain polyunsaturated fatty acids) or omega-3 oils, which are now added to formula to promote brain, eye and nerve growth. In many ways, it's

While all the positive aspects of breastfeeding are meant to encourage women to consider it for themselves, it should not lead to bouts of guilt and anguish for those who have tried their very best but aren't able to do it.[34] Especially when you are anxious and exhausted, the most insignificant remark, as seen above (often well-meant but nonetheless condescending), destroys your confidence and makes your determination waver.

We are up against a combination of factors that can affect us all to differing extents. They are varied and very often beyond our control. Physiological factors brought on by a traumatic birth experience, and birth interventions, are amongst them. Even if the mother has to undergo a minor operation such as an appendectomy when her baby is still very young can interfere with well-intentioned plans. The same applies to premature babies who might have problems latching on correctly, or babies born with

---

simply too soon to know what effect DHA (docosahexaenoic acid)- and ARA (arachidonic acid)-supplemented formula will have on brain development. These compounds may play a role in decreasing allergic and respiratory diseases, but at the same time it is important to note that the primary reason (and major marketing ploy) behind the addition of these supplements is visual and central nervous system development – something for which we will have to wait and see: https://www.fda.gov/food/foodborneillnesscontaminants/ peopleatrisk/ucm108079.htm#16. However, babies will be able to assimilate these essential fats when weaned in the form of fish and/ or flaxseed oil. Weaning them should be as close to six months as possible (see Tip 5 for more information on this).

34  For a more balanced view, though this won't mean carte blanche: http://www.bbc.com/future/story/20170503-are- there-downsides-to-breast-is-best ; https://www.thedailybeast. com/the-breast-is-best-breastfeeding-campaign-is-misguided and https://www.health.harvard.edu/blog/why-we-shouldnt- demonize-formula-feeding-2018040313557

a cleft palate or ankyloglossia (tongue-tie).[35] Cultural factors, such as the overly sexualised perception of female bodies, and breasts in particular, are part of the problem too. Couple these with prudish attitudes such as anxiety about offending other people when feeding in public (see Tip 3), or fears of potential child abuse accusations when co-sleeping/bedsharing, and you have several triggers and some powerful psychological conditioning which most of us won't be able to resist. The feeling that it is somehow wrong or offensive to feed in public or with other people other than our partner present will always be at the bottom of our actions, and will make us an easy target for the marketing interests of formula companies. Let's have a look at a few of the facts.

## Feeding on the breast: its strong points

The World Health Organization (WHO) recommends exclusive breastfeeding for the first six months, and breastfeeding alongside solids for up to two years.[36] If this seems like an unbelievably long time which won't fit in with anything you expected your life or even parenthood to be and you are struggling to make up your mind, it is essential to note that differences between breast milk and formula are significant not only nutritionally, but also psychologically.

Let's start with the nutritional side of things. Breast milk contains at least thirty-four ingredients (see Table 1

---

35  This is when the strip of skin connecting the tip of the tongue to the floor of the mouth is shorter than usual:
https://www.nhs.uk/conditions/tongue-tie/

36  https://www.who.int/news-room/fact-sheets/detail/infant-and-young-child-feeding#targetText=WHO%20and%20UNICEF%20recommend%3A,years%20of%20age%20or%20beyond.

below), such as antibodies, certain types of fats etc. not found in formula, which needs to be processed from cow's milk to make it digestible for your growing baby. The very first milk your body produces for your baby is called colostrum, which is so potent that it works like an early immunisation to protect this new life and make it stronger, which, however, does not mean that there is no need for vaccination (see Tip 23)[37]. The benefits of colostrum cannot be replaced by formula. In simple terms, breast milk primes your baby's gut and immune system for lifelong health.

Even the size of the thymus gland is related to the number of breastfeeds a day, and in breastfed babies can be double the size of that of an artificially fed baby.[38] This gland controls the development of our immune response.[39] This becomes especially apparent in artificially fed babies being more prone to suffering from respiratory, gastrointestinal and ear infections, and obesity, in later life.[40] Another exciting aspect is the greater quantity of so-called white matter, essential for carrying nerve impulses between neurons in the brain, in breastfed babies as their brains develop, which impacts on the child's IQ.[41]

---

37  Read more on this particular issue: https://www.vaccinestoday.eu/faq/babies-receive-antibodies-with-breast-milk-why-do-they-need-vaccines-if-they-already-get-this-natural-protection/

38  Lars A. Hanson, *Immunobiology of Human Milk: How Breastfeeding Protects Babies* (2004).

39  P. T. Ngom et al., 'Improved thymic function in exclusively breastfed babies is associated with higher interleukin 7 concentrations in their mothers' breast milk' in *American Journal of Clinical Nutrition* 2004, Sep 1, 80 (3): 722-28.

40  A. Koch et al., 'Risk factors for acute respiratory tract infections in young Greenlandic children' in *American Journal of Epidemiology* 2003, Aug 15, 158 (4): 374–84.

41  E. B. Isaacs et al., 'Impact of breast milk on intelligence quotient,

The National Childbirth Trust (NCT)[42] also lists benefits for yourself, such as a lower risk of Type 2 diabetes, if you breastfeed for up to six months.

| BREAST MILK | FORMULA |
|---|---|
| Growth factors (help with growth and development) | / |
| White cells (help protect against infection) | / |
| Antibodies (help protect against infection) | / |
| Viral fragments (promote immunity) | / |
| Immunoglobins (promote immunity) | / |
| Transfer factors (help ensure nutrients are absorbed) | / |
| Hormones (help control how cells and organs function) | / |
| Enzymes (aid digestion and destroy harmful bacteria) | / |
| Oligosaccharides (fats that promote gut health) | / |

---

brain size, and white matter development' in *Pediatric Research* 2010, Apr 1, 67 (4): 357–62. To take this even further, some researchers argue that changes in the human microbiome, i.e. the unique composition of bacteria, viruses and fungi within us, are likely to affect subsequent generations as regards obesity and inflammatory and autoimmune diseases (see A. Wakeford and T. Harman, *The Microbiome Effect* [2016]). This is mainly due to greater processed food consumption – and it all starts with formula.

42  https://www.nct.org.uk/

| Bifidus factor (sounds a bit like yoghurt – it promotes gut health) | / |
|---|---|
| Vitamins and minerals | Vitamins and minerals |
| Carbohydrate | Carbohydrate |
| Fat | Fat |
| Water | Water |
| Protein | Protein |

Table 1: *Breast Milk vs Formula: Nutritional Value*
Source: *Off to a Good Start* (NHS Scotland, 2016,
http://www.healthscotland.scot)

## What do I need to breastfeed?

A Google search gives you about 9,030,000 results if you type in this question. I have looked. Seriously. But in vain: breasts weren't on the list.

Joking aside, you certainly won't need as many items of equipment as with bottle-feeding, but some things are helpful. You will need a cotton nursing bra with a clip. Get one fitted at thirty-seven weeks, by which time your breasts might even be starting to leak a bit of colostrum, and then again when your baby is about two to three weeks old and your milk has come in. Because bras need to be comfortable, it is best to buy them in store to get them fitted. You may also need pads if your breasts are leaking, but this varies according to the individual. Frequent nursing is likely to prevent leaking. If you do need pads, try to get washable ones.[43]

---

43  Try Little Lamb washable bamboo nursing pads. These are washable for up to fifty times, antimicrobial and breathable: https://littlelambnappies.com/products/

Another thing you most likely won't be able to do without is an ointment to help with sore and cracked nipples. Weleda and Lansinoh[44] are brilliant in this respect, and you won't even have to wipe it off before the next feed. Air your breasts in front of the fire or let the sun shine on them, discreetly and according to season. Nipples that are already sore can easily become chafed when covered in layers of clothing. A remedy that is completely DIY is your own breastmilk. Rub some of your own expressed breast milk onto the affected areas – it does do wonders, I have tried.

You might want to invest in a breast pump, depending on your situation. You have a choice between manual and different models of electric breast pumps, and also the option to express by hand.[45] I too thought I needed a pump, before my midwife said to me that I shouldn't buy anything just yet. And I never did. I am still so glad I followed her advice as it prevented me from adding any more clutter to my kitchen.

Apart from costing you a lot of money and adding to the stuff in your home, these breastfeeding products also have risks and can negatively impact your milk supply. If you can get your full maternity leave, which hopefully you will[46], you're not likely to need a pump.

---

bamboo-breast-pads?gclid=EAIaIQobChMI-sT8-v3z5QIVB7LtCh3l2wEyEAAYASAAEgJ-ifD_BwE

44 https://www.weleda.co.uk/ and https://lansinoh.co.uk/

45 For more information refer to La Leche League's *Sweet Sleep* (2014) (chapter on hand expression or breast pumps), and/or see your breastfeeding consultant.

46 Make sure you find out about your rights before you go off work. You can start here: https://www.gov.uk/maternity-pay-leave and speak to your midwife and other health professionals or your local

Newly expectant parents often purchase these things as a matter of course, but expressing is different from your baby suckling on your breast. You might even find that they refuse a bottle the longer you have breastfed them.[47] It is even worse to think that there are gadgets (and that is what they are) such as MilkSense[48] to measure your breast milk output, or Happy Vitals,[49] which is supposed to analyse the content of your breast milk to ascertain if your baby is actually getting the right "stuff". These types of machines will unnecessarily interfere with a perfectly natural process which is well beyond its first trial run. It has been fully functional for millions of years, in fact, as long as mammals have been around on planet Earth, which is for about 210 million years[50]. You have got your best indicator right there: a growing baby. Wet nappies. Poopy nappies. That is all the evidence you need, and do trust your own judgement. How did the human species ever get to this point without all of that machinery?! Or put it the other way: just look at the mess we are in with nonsense like that.

Whether you choose to purchase some of the equipment depends mainly on your thoughts about going back to work, which is often a necessity if the running of the household relies on two wages coming

---

Citizen's Advice Bureau who will be able to give you some useful information on these matters.

47  For more on this, go to Amy Brown's chapter on technology and breastfeeding in her book *Breastfeeding Uncovered* (2016) (see Recommended Reading).

48  https://www.arkitd.com/project/milk-sense/ ; https://mymomsense.com/

49  https://angel.co/happyvitals

50  http://www.bobpickett.org/evolution_of_mammals.htm

in or if you are a single parent. In these cases, if you express your baby won't have to miss out on breast milk, although one has to bear in mind that for lactational amenorrhoea to kick in, a woman needs to be exclusively breastfeeding for the first five to six months.[51] This is also called ecological breastfeeding.[52] It involves feeding your baby with only your milk for about six months, on demand, day and night. Ban the use of any soothers. At six months, you can move on to a gradual introduction of small amounts of selected foods, while continuing to breastfeed your baby as their first food for about one year or longer. The baby's frequent and prolonged suckling causes your level of prolactin (a hormone which causes you to lactate properly) to remain reasonably high.[53] It won't be as high as after giving birth, when the progesterone and oestrogen levels take a sudden dip post-partum, and prolactin rises as a consequence. This happens after delivery when you need your milk to come in, but, as time passes, the levels are usually still high enough to prevent you from ovulating. This has, at least potentially, a positive effect on natural birth control or child spacing.[54] For it to work as a means of natural birth control, the scientific consensus is that frequency and the total duration of breastfeeding are the most substantial determining factors.[55] You will already be able to gauge

---

51  https://www.ncbi.nlm.nih.gov/pubmed/9678098

52  https://www.ncbi.nlm.nih.gov/pubmed/3042247

53  https://www.ncbi.nlm.nih.gov/pubmed/2092340

54  For more information see https://modernalternativemama. com/2014/02/18/ecological-breastfeeding-a-natural-approach-to-child-spacing/

55  https://kellymom.com/ages/older-infant/fertility/

the return of your fertility based on changes in your cervical mucus.[56] On average, in women who breastfeed exclusively for six months, and who go on to continue night feeds and frequent feeding throughout the day after introducing solids, periods return after 14.6 months.[57] In some women, ovulation can resume perhaps before the first menstrual bleeding, and this is more the case the longer lactation lasts.[58]

I would also advise against nipple shields if you can help it as the best thing, once again, is to air your nipples as much as possible and bear the discomfort of any cracking, which is very likely to subside within about two weeks. The problem with nipple shields is that they prevent direct skin contact while your baby is suckling, and hence your body responds with lower oxytocin levels. Think of somebody kissing you with a protective shield! Therefore, your baby can extract less milk per feed.[59] In some cases, however, shields can be useful; for example, with premature babies who have problems latching on. And the best remedy against initial discomfort is: feed your baby. You need to keep feeding to get used to it. Sticking cold cabbage leaves into your bra to relieve tender, engorged breasts is a well-known, about-as-green-as-you-can-get remedy, although the best way is to prevent engorgement by frequent feeding, which should generally bring relief.

---

56  https://www.mamanatural.com/cervical-mucus/

57  https://kellymom.com/ages/older-infant/fertility/

58  https://kellymom.com/ages/older-infant/fertility/

59  K. G. Auerbach, 'The effect of nipple shields on maternal milk volume' in *Journal of Obstetric, Gynecologic & Neonatal Nursing* 1990, Sep 1; 19 (5): 419–30.

| GOOD AND EASY | PERHAPS SOMEWHAT OF A NUISANCE |
|---|---|
| Ideal nutrition for your baby. Think of breast milk as the perfect food: it's always the right temperature and is sterile. | Initial discomfort. |
| Infection-fighting and healthy as it leads to a lower risk of many diseases such as eczema, ear infections and childhood obesity. | Initial time investment. |
| It is the healthiest option for you too. It helps with post-partum weight loss. You burn an extra 500 calories a day, and this will help you regain your figure sooner. Breastfeeding is also associated with a lower risk of menopausal breast cancer. | Dietary restrictions: alcohol, caffeine, and perhaps 'windy' foods such as cabbage and raw milk products because of strains of bacteria such as listeria, which can potentially be harmful to your baby. As a guideline, most of the foods that were on the red list while you were pregnant should be treated with caution while breastfeeding as well. |
| Bonding. | |
| Environmentally friendly: no packaging, no plastic bottles, no production waste and no transport. | |

| | |
|---|---|
| Convenient: you don't have to sterilise bottles and make up feeds; it is always ready to go. | |
| Reduced menstruation, so-called lactational amenorrhoea (LAM), i.e. delayed return of fertility, which gives your body more time to recover. | |
| Cheaper: no need to buy expensive bottle equipment, formula, sterilisers, bottle warmers – the list goes on! | |

Table 2: *Breastfeeding*

As we can see from Table 2, discomfort and time investment are perhaps a consideration, but they will soon be a distant memory. You are actually going to have more time on your hands once breastfeeding has been successfully established. The health benefits, both for your child and for yourself, clearly stand in its favour. The bonding and the delayed return of your fertility are bonuses which only add to your overall physical and mental health. And last but not least, there is also a financial incentive to continue with breastfeeding instead of switching to formula if you can help it. If you breastfeed for up to a year, you'll save an estimated £450 by not buying formula, bottles, sterilisers etc.

# Feeding with formula: is it so much easier and more convenient?

| GOOD AND EASY | PERHAPS SOMEWHAT OF A NUISANCE |
|---|---|
| Fewer feeds in 24 hours. | The kettle boiled at least 900 times to make up a feed. |
| You can measure your baby's milk intake. | 50 non-recyclable packs of formula powder (900g each). |
| Easier when going back to work. | Steriliser run up to 360 times (twice daily). |
| No dietary restrictions for yourself. | Having to buy and use plastic bottles and teats. |
| | Wasted milk poured down the sink. |
| | Getting frazzled stumbling into the kitchen at 3am to prepare a feed for an infant in distress. |

Table 3: *Formula (Source: K. Blincoe [2016])*
Figures based on an estimated average of five 210 ml (7 fl. oz) feeds per day for six months.

What about a bottle-feeding scenario? No disturbed sleep? Honestly? I have never tried, but stumbling down the stairs into the kitchen, making up a feed, checking it's the right temperature, by which time I am fully awake, hubby very probably is too and the baby is crying in distress – none of this ever seemed very appealing to me. Breastfeeding, I never needed to worry about any of that. My daughter stirred in her sleep, I pulled her towards me, lying on my side, and let her find the breast. I also managed to drift back to sleep relatively quickly thanks to the hormone oxytocin, which your body produces while breastfeeding and which makes you nicely relaxed and sleepy.[60]

As becomes fairly apparent from the advantages and disadvantages listed in Tables 2 and 3, the use of formula will first and foremost enable you to return to your old life as quickly as possible, which might very often be the whole point. Alleged convenience is another thing. On the other hand, you are probably going to make more trips to the local GP's surgery with your baby if you feed them formula, because it is nutritionally less complete than breast milk and your baby is likely to be ill more often or to recover less swiftly from minor ailments. Babies are also more likely to develop colic if fed on formula. It is time-consuming in being prepared, and even higher in cost. Overall, it is worth a second thought as far as convenience is concerned.

Let's have a look at the time aspect. Amy Brown was able to report the following stats: 18.2 hours went into exclusive breastfeeding as opposed to 11.6 hours into formula. Including preparation when solids have been introduced, the figures would be brought up to 18.7 hours for the breastfed baby and 15.4 hours for the formula-fed baby. But here is the flip side: breastfeeding mums got more help with general care, perhaps because if one task such as feeding the baby gets split between different parties others will as well, such as doing the dishes and the laundry – 324 minutes compared with 235 minutes for those who feed formula.[61] In this sense, time cannot be the incentive.

---

60  http://www.infantjournal.co.uk/pdf/inf_054_ers.pdf; also see http://www.kerstinuvnasmoberg.com/

61  A. Brown, *Breastfeeding Uncovered*, Chapter 4, loc. 2697.

## I am struggling – where can I get support?

Despite all of the above, the Breast is Best[62] campaign should not infringe on a mother's right to choose what she feels is best for herself and her baby. The crux of the matter is that we aren't really in a situation where we can choose freely. We find too many obstacles in our way.

Moreover, there are mighty market forces at work. Despite the International Code of Marketing Breastmilk Substitutes[63] instituted in 1981 by the WHO to ban the promotion of breast milk substitutes for babies under six months, adverts for formula are broadcast on TV during a crucial time slot, i.e. when young families are likely to watch.[64] The essential element of the code is the restriction of substitutes being promoted to the parents of very young babies; hence it does not include other types of formula food such as follow-on formula, which have only been invented to circumvent these restrictions. And as long as powerful companies such as Nestlé have a vested interest in promoting their products, they are likely to continue doing so – at a high human and environmental cost.

Seek out local breastfeeding support groups if you are struggling. The NHS offers free breastfeeding classes along with their antenatal classes. A valuable source of information is La Leche League.[65] Depending on where you live, you may be able to attend local meetings. You

---

62 https://betterbreastfeeding.uk/2017/08/06/better-breastfeeding-a-new-campaign-is-launched/

63 https://www.unicef.org.uk/babyfriendly/baby-friendly-resources/international-code-marketing-breastmilk-substitutes-resources/the-code/

64 http://www.babymilkaction.org/ukrules-pt2a

65 https://www.laleche.org.uk

can have a look at their website and also order their book, which contains lots of good ideas, troubleshooting advice and encouragement.

## Ask the expert: Jenny Walker, breastfeeding peer support coordinator

Jenny is blonde, slender and calm. She also looks a lot younger than her age. Don't be deceived by that, though. Together with only two colleagues she covers the whole of Dumfries and Galloway, working as a breastfeeding consultant employed by the NHS. A devoted and caring mother herself, she speaks from the heart and is passionate about helping other women on their journey to a joyful breastfeeding relationship with their babies. She runs antenatal breastfeeding classes and a Mum2Mum breastfeeding support group in Castle Douglas on Thursday afternoons.

I first met her when I was nine months pregnant and listening to her expertise in one of her classes. Although in my case she did not have much convincing to do – I knew that I wanted to breastfeed – I still wanted to hear more about it, because nobody had told me what I needed to know and the women in my family (my mother, stepmother and aunts) either hadn't breastfed for very long or didn't have any children of their own.

When I arrived at the GP's surgery, I was surprised to see that only another two mums-to-be apart from myself had turned up to attend Jenny's class. There had been six heavily pregnant women in the other antenatal classes, where they talk to you about the onset of labour, what to look out for when the time comes, items you will need to pack in your and your baby's hospital bags, and hospital procedures. After the class, I had asked one of the other mums-to-be if she was considering going to the breastfeeding talk later that afternoon. She shrugged. Earlier, she had asked the midwife if she had to bring formula and bottles to the birthing suite to have everything at hand. I remember looking at her, amazed and a little shocked at the same time. So, when I asked her, her reply was, after the non-committal shrug, "Well, people do say it's disgusting, a baby sucking on your breast. I don't think I'm going to, really." Unfortunately, this illustrates the situation all too well.

But it is best if we let Jenny speak for herself.

*How do you support women with breastfeeding problems?*

Women with breastfeeding problems are vulnerable. It is important we give them self-belief and empower them during this time.

They have had a baby and their emotions are running high. They might be feeling sore from the delivery and sleep-deprived. They are also receiving conflicting advice on parenthood on top of trying to learn how to breastfeed. This is an emotional time.

Women need a good listener, non-judgemental guidance and time to receive gentle advice and education to help them through this (at times tricky) stage.

The early days can be difficult. The majority of breastfeeding problems at this time come from poor positioning and attachment. If good support and guidance is given to the mother, then hopefully she will gain confidence in herself as a new mum, and in breastfeeding her baby.

I like to give women time and reassurance during the early days. They can be quick to give up if no support is given during this time.

Following women through their breastfeeding journey is lovely, and I have built some great relationships over time. The breastfeeding support group also helps 'normalise' breastfeeding and gives women the chance to make friends who also have babies.

*What are the commonest problems?*

I believe the most common problems are:

- "Is my baby getting enough?"
- "My nipples are sore!"

Educating antenatally is so important. If women have an idea of what to expect in the early days, then when baby arrives there is a better understanding of why a baby feeds frequently, tummy size, and good positioning and attachment. It is imperative that this is reinforced when the baby arrives. If women can get off to a good start with breastfeeding, then they will hopefully have minimal issues like sore nipples, poor lactation, poor weight gain in baby... The list goes on.

Breastfeeding should be pain free. It is normal to feel a bit bruised – our breasts are a sensitive area – but pain can be avoided if the right support is given from delivery.

*Why do we have such low success rates for breastfeeding in the UK?*

I believe there are a few factors that contribute to this:

LACK OF EDUCATION: Nobody is breastfeeding in the soaps on TV, and it gets no promotion via adverts. So how can it be seen as 'normal'? The benefits of breastfeeding for mothers and babies are unknown to many in the UK today. I find that very frustrating. Educating everyone through TV, radio etc. is so important. We need to normalise breastfeeding so everyone out there accepts it. It should be seen as the most natural thing for a mother to do; women should not face negative pressure from society when they have chosen to do the best thing possible for their babies.

EMBARRASSMENT: Women are afraid to breastfeed due to the opinions and lack of education of other people in society today. They don't feel they can comfortably breastfeed in front of anyone because they will be judged.

TIME: Life is fast, and more women are working now, unlike in the 'old days'. So I think to get women to take the time out to sit for prolonged periods feeding… Well, they aren't always prepared to do it. Many women talk about 'mixed feeding', so that others can also feed the baby. I discuss the importance of only the parents feeding the baby if using a bottle, for bonding and relationship building, during the breastfeeding workshops.

CULTURE: Some women may be from formula-feeding families, so it is difficult to break the tradition. Getting women to attend a breastfeeding class is tricky if their families are influencing them in the background.

FORMULA: The adverts on TV are so clever. "Forty years of research, which makes formula as close to breast milk..." so women then think that formula is as good as breast milk. Formula will never have the immunity factors that protect a baby. But advertising is powerful.

LACK OF SUPPORT: There aren't always good breastfeeding resources for women to access. If they cannot get support in the early days and have little education on the subject, then they give up. The breastfeeding support drop-ins are so good for women. The peer support you can find there is so beneficial. I would encourage *all* breastfeeding women to attend one if possible.

*So how can this be corrected?*

I believe that *Education + Time + Support = Success.*

The NHS, government etc. need to start providing better resources in order for women to have success with breastfeeding. Breastfeeding support is needed antenatally for education, and then should be available from birth onwards. All experiences are different, and a holistic approach should be used for every woman.

*Why do some women choose not to breastfeed?*

Lack of education about the health benefits, cultural reasons, sexualisation of breasts (they aren't considered to be 'for babies'), embarrassment, 'help' with feeding baby, going back to work early, negative attitudes from friends and family, medication and so on…

I say to people that it is easier to give breastfeeding a try, than to look back and wish they had given it a go, but by then it's too late. Women need to take a step back and realise that their baby needs them. I mean, what is more important than your baby?

Surrender yourself to your baby and accept that breastfeeding is a commitment which gives your baby the best start possible in life. Bonding with and nurturing your child is the most rewarding job in the world. The benefits are huge!

Breastfeeding is so empowering for a woman – we are built to give birth and provide amazing health benefits by breastfeeding our children. I appreciate breastfeeding isn't for everyone, but I feel we could improve people's attitudes greatly if we promoted breastfeeding, and educated and empowered everyone properly. We have to normalise breastfeeding in the UK. I feel formula advertising should be restricted or removed from TV as it gives women false information. Formula will never give the immunity breast milk provides, so it should not be advertised like it's the equivalent of breast milk.

## And what if all else fails?

Try googling "breastfeeding failure". When I did it in January 2020, it brought up 23 Million results. It just brings it home to us what a terrible predicament we are in. The pressure goes both ways – no matter if you choose to breastfeed or if you have made up your mind that you won't because of work commitments or simply because you don't have a choice as a single mum and your job is the only source of income. And if it is your choice, chances are you will have made up your mind and you are hopefully comfortable with it.

But what if you wanted to do it so very badly and you cannot? Finding yourself in such a situation can be extremely hard on everybody involved, including other family members and friends. You may experience fears and feelings of failure believing you are not being able to provide the very best for your baby. This can taint the whole experience of motherhood and adversely affect even the strongest of relationships.

There can be various reasons why breastfeeding is not only difficult but near enough impossible for some as I have discussed above and I will give a few more examples as you read along. After all, there is a point when acceptance is the key and trying to make the best of it. Those of us who have undergone the trials and tribulations of IVF (in-vitro-fertilisation) know about this.

If you are reading this while you are still pregnant, make sure you find out what kind of support you have access to.

Start with your mind set and examine your fears even before your baby arrives. Remind yourself that pregnancy, birth and breastfeeding are natural processes. Book a session with a breastfeeding consultant you can fall back on to when needed if there is likely to be a lack of support in your direct environment. Speak openly about your concerns. The initial decision to breastfeed and your determination are key.

Then, there are ways to feed your baby supplement formula from a pouch with a small tube you place on your breast. These things are called "nursing supplementers"[66]

---

66  https://www.laleche.org.uk/nursing-supplementers/

and I have seen them in use with a friend and her baby. When using these, your baby will still suckle on your breast and be supplemented with formula at the same time. And then, most importantly, there is your presence and your closeness that matters. You can still co-sleep and chances are that breastfeeding will come easier to you and your baby if you decide to co-sleep.

Also, it is not your fault. You are not a failure. You can still do all the other wonderful things that are vital ingredients of mothering, which are to play and sing and read stories, even if you need to stop breastfeeding before you wanted to or never got off to a good start. The most important thing is the initial willingness to do it and accepting it for what it is – the natural extension of pregnancy and giving birth as a mammal. As will be discussed below (Tip 3) we are in a situation in which we are faced with too many difficult obstacles in our way which overcomplicate it and often lead to failure. This is unfortunately true with attempts to achieve a straightforward delivery as well as breastfeeding. It will get easier along the way. And now, I won't hold back any longer, so read on.

# TIP 2
## Establish Your Milk Supply by Baby-Led Feeding

*Sorry, what? Feeding my baby on demand?*
*What does my baby know about economics?*

Baby-led feeding is also known as demand feeding or responsive feeding. So what is meant by this? It means, quite simply, that your baby will ask for what they need, and your milk production will respond. The production of milk will naturally fluctuate according to your baby's needs. It works by responding promptly to baby's feeding cues in the first few weeks to establish your milk supply. It is all based on a very personal interaction. It may often seem to you as though your baby is still being born and only about to evolve into the person they are one day going to be.[67] So, what do you and others (health professionals, partners, family) need to do to get there?

Following the Innocenti Declaration of 1990, which outlines the Ten Steps to Successful Breastfeeding, UNICEF launched their Baby-Friendly Hospital Initiative (BFHI) in 1991. By 2004, nineteen thousand hospitals in 150 countries had gained BF (Baby Friendly) status.[68] BFHI policies include undisturbed skin-to-skin contact for at least an hour after birth, rooming-in and controlled use of formula. All of these (and more) were implemented to facilitate breastfeeding and help mothers and babies. Even if it is medically indicated to help you along with the birthing process (and with a hospital birth it is more than likely that a reason will be found, however small), all is not lost if we give some thought to the following:

THE 'MAGIC HOUR': It used to be routine hospital procedure to whisk babies off to a nursery so that mothers could rest following delivery. Unlike just one or two generations ago,

---

67  This is why this period is often referred to as the fourth trimester: https://www.babycentre.co.uk/a25019365/your-baby-and-the-fourth-trimester

68  https://www.who.int/nutrition/publications/infantfeeding/9789241594998_s4.pdf

it is now common practice in most hospitals to leave babies with their mothers, unless a medical emergency prevents this. This means that the process of separation is less sudden, and the practice is known as 'rooming-in'.[69] More importantly, immediately after birth babies are now placed on their mother's chest for warmth and skin-to-skin contact. When this happens with as little delay as possible, the baby will instinctively search for the breast. Newborn mammals are instinctively programmed to find the 'teat'. Babies are capable of doing all the work; they crawl up to the breast. This phenomenon is known as the 'breast crawl', and was first described in 1987 at the Karolinska Institute in Sweden, where they were able to observe it in babies who were placed on their mothers' legs directly after birth.[70] Some examples of this have been recorded and can be watched on YouTube.[71]

CORRECT ATTACHMENT: Breastfeeding consultants, nurses, midwives – everybody will talk to you about this. It means that your baby should take in as much of the breast as they can into their tiny mouth, not just the nipple. What they are supposed to be doing is massaging the milk ducts; that is what squeezes the milk out, not the sucking and pulling on the nipple. Once they have got the hang of it, this is also very likely to prevent soreness, although you are bound to feel some real discomfort to start with. Don't despair; it will subside.

---

69  For more information on keeping mother and baby together see: https://www.ncbi.nlm.nih.gov/pmc/articles/PMC4235060/; https://pediatrics.aappublications.org/content/pediatrics/early/2016/08/18/peds.2016-1889.full.pdf
70  http://breastcrawl.org/science.shtml.
71  https://www.youtube.com/watch?v=0OYXd-mMSVU

FEEDING WHEN THE BABY DISPLAYS CUES: These cues are known as rooting, stirring and, as a last resort, crying. In real life, it is not possible to prevent a baby from crying every time they get hungry. But learning how to read their cues and responding swiftly to them is often referred to as 'demand feeding', even though I think 'baby-led feeding' or 'responsive feeding' describe the process a whole lot better. For this, you need to be able to interpret your baby's cues, and you shouldn't be trying to feed them according to a superimposed schedule. Until a generation or two ago, and sometimes even to this day, young mothers were told to feed every four hours and switch from one breast to the other after ten minutes.[72] This practice is not advisable for various reasons. It will not only interfere with your milk supply, but may also cause long-term negative psychological effects for you and your baby. The notion of making even the feeding of babies more efficient may well have been introduced to make better use of women as part of a cheap industrial workforce. For women higher up the social ladder, the aim might have been to free them up for 'important' social engagements.[73]

FEEDING FOR AS LONG AS BABY WANTS TO: Yes, please do. What would you think if you were interrupted continuously when having your favourite meal, the plate snatched away from you right in front of your eyes? Be positive: feeding times will reduce over time, as will the number of feeds in a twenty-four-hour period. It is an erroneous

---

72 https://www.emmapickettbreastfeedingsupport.com/twitter-and-blog/the-dangerous-game-of-the-feeding-interval-obsession

73 https://en.wikipedia.org/wiki/Eight-hour_day

notion that frequent feeds mean there isn't enough milk – although in a sense it does mean that. Your baby feeds that often to let you know that they need more milk, to which your body promptly responds by producing more of it. Once that has been established, feeding frenzies will settle down again. This is what makes your baby grow and fills them up, so you don't want to switch them over after ten minutes, which will deprive them of a proper feed. If they wish to nurse on the other side, they will let you know. I used a ring which I would swap onto the other hand, depending on which side I needed to feed my baby from next. I found this method very helpful as a reminder. A little ribbon on your bra strap might work equally well.

LEARN TO FEED IN DIFFERENT POSITIONS AND HOLDS: This means that sitting in a slightly reclined position propped up with hundreds of cushions is not the only way to do it. Try to feed while holding your baby with a pillow for support under your elbow, sitting cross-legged on the floor, lying on your side on a bed or a duvet on the rug; even as you gently walk about or sit and hold a book or send texts from your mobile (yes, that's all right too). It's all about not ending up sitting in a chair all day. As the feeds become shorter and perhaps fewer, and both of you grow more accomplished at feeding, then this is the way to go.

You are also likely to be told, or to read, that your baby is expected to feed about eight to twelve times daily in the first few weeks. In my experience, this was nonsense. My baby would feed randomly to begin with and whenever

I was asked (usually by older family members who had used formula), I was never able to tell how often. It just felt like all the time. And I decided it didn't matter, because she got fed, and that was what mattered. Given that it is best for you to rest and recover, it has to be possible to make time for it when your baby needs you. We are talking about a few weeks, not a considerable amount of time in the grand scheme of things. Your daily feeding schedule is likely going to drop to six to nine times by the second month. According to a Swedish study, eleven to twelve daily feeds are normal; then they drop, only to increase again at twenty weeks.[74] The !Kung in South Africa feed their babies frequently, often for only a few minutes at a time, sometimes four times an hour and for less than two minutes on average, with thirteen minutes in between.[75] Looking at the content of human milk, this all makes sense. Amy Brown makes the point that it is relatively low in fat and protein, and digested quickly, which means your baby needs to feed frequently. Just think of their tiny stomach, which is only the size of a cherry on the day they are born and about the size of an egg by the time they are a month old.[76] Of course they grow hungry again quickly. The baby-led nature of breastfeeding is thought to facilitate appetite regulation as the baby is more in control of the

74  A. Hörnell et al., 'Breastfeeding patterns in exclusively breastfed infants: a longitudinal prospective study in Uppsala, Sweden' in *Acta Paediatrica* 1999, Feb 1; 88 (2): 203–11.

75  M. Konner and C. Worthman, 'Nursing frequency, gonadal function, and birth spacing among !Kung hunter-gatherers' in *Science* 1980, Feb 15; 207 (4432): 788–91.

76  NHS Scotland, *Off to a Good Start: All You Need to Know About Breastfeeding* (2018, p. 31).

amount consumed[77]. Learning to "listen" to their own bodies this way will help them control their food intake in later life.[78] As you will see in Tip 4, so is waking up, which is directly related to feeding and is vital for their immature nervous system.[79]

One way of telling that you're on the right track is if your baby is producing up to eight heavy, wet cloth nappies a day. If you want to see what that feels like, pour about four tablespoons of water on them. Ask your midwife or health visitor for information on what the stool in the first few days is supposed to look like until it turns into the ordinary grainy-mustard-coloured type. This is quite runny too, which is to be expected for a breastfed baby and is probably easiest for their immature bowels to process. It will change to something more solid later, by the time they are about six months old and starting to take some solid food.[80]

---

77  https://onlinelibrary.wiley.com/doi/abs/10.1111/j.2047-6310.2012.00071.x; https://www.ncbi.nlm.nih.gov/pubmed/22911888

78  A. Brown and M. Lee, 'Breastfeeding during the first year promotes satiety responsiveness in children aged 18–24 months' in *Pediatric Obesity* 2012, Oct 1; 7 (5): 382–90. If you are anxious about your baby's weight loss or gain, I recommend reading Chapter 2 in Amy Brown's *Breastfeeding Uncovered* (2016).

79  S. Mosko, C. Richard and J. McKenna, 'Maternal sleep and arousals during bedsharing with infants' in *Sleep* 1997, 20 (2): 142–50 and S. Mosko, C. Richard and J. McKenna, 'Infant arousals during mother-infant bed sharing: implications for infant sleep and sudden infant death syndrome research' in *Pediatrics* 1997, 100 (5): 841–849.

80  For more information go straight to Tips 5 and 6.

# TIP 3

## Let Your Baby Have Their Meal in Public – and Take Them With You Everywhere You Go

*Do I need to cover myself? And what is green about this?*

Who won't remember the media frenzy around the woman who so very shockingly had her meal at Claridge's and decided to give her little one a feed too?[81] Or the women ostentatiously breastfeeding as a form of protest in Sports Direct stores across the country?[82]

In response to the Claridge's row, Jeremy Clarkson famously remarked that 'breastfeeding is natural… just like urinating'.[83] He would maybe be interested to hear that, quite intriguingly, lactation doesn't only occur after having given birth. Some mammals can lactate and nurture the young of other females.[84] And quite astonishingly, even the human male can lactate. Recently, a so-called 'chestfeeding' kit went viral in the news.[85] This contraption was designed by Marie-Claire Springham to stimulate the let-down reflex in men. All of this isn't going to work, however, unless the expectant dad is prepared to

81  https://www.theguardian.com/lifeandstyle/2014/dec/02/claridges-hotel-breastfeeding-woman-cover-up

82  https://www.bbc.co.uk/news/uk-england-27253488

83  https://www.indy100.com/article/guess-what-most-people-support-breastfeeding-in-public--gyfBRvqktl

84  S. Jones, *Almost Like a Whale: The Origin of Species Updated* (1999) and H. Marieskind, 'Abnormal lactation' in *Journal of Tropical Pediatrics and Environmental Child Health* 1973, 19: 123–28.

85  http://www.ladbible.com/news/weird-new-hormone-kit-could-make-it-possible-for-men-breastfeed-20181025

take hormones to grow 'milk ducts' and so-called 'moobs' (which, rather unimaginatively, is a contraction of 'man boobs'). When I mentioned this to my husband, he looked briefly over my shoulder as I was writing and then turned around and said, "That's enough!" and quickly left the room. Here we are, then! Try and tell male friends and family members, and your partner, for that matter, if you want to cause the most emancipated share-all-the-household-chores and paternity-leave-and-let-her-get-on-with-her-career type of guy to squeamishly avert his eyes and squirm and fidget uncomfortably.

Anyway, have you ever asked yourself why the human female has breasts which are indeed very large compared to those of our closest relatives, the great apes, even when not lactating? It is quite possible that human breasts emerged as an evolutionary response to our walking on two legs.[86] As our spines and pelvises adjusted to this innovation, a cleavage that resembled our backside was required upfront to attract the opposite sex. But let's face it: breasts secrete milk. That is their primary function. There still seems to be a lot of prejudice against this in the Western world, and perhaps of late it has even been on the rise due to how sexualised breasts have become. This is one of the reasons why we find little breastfeeding cubicles next to the toilet areas in some places.[87] Just stop and think for a minute – why should that be necessary? In this way, breastfeeding is being degraded to something we should do in private, like other bodily functions.

---

86  https://www.psychologytoday.com/intl/blog/sex-dawn/201004/why-do-breasts-mesmerize

87  This is, for example, the case in the brand-new hospital in Dumfries, Scotland.

Amy Brown quite rightly points out that it is not about the mother's actions. We need to see breastfeeding as a biologically normal response to a baby needing to feed.[88] You are not required to expose your breasts for all to see; there are ways and means to nurse and still feel comfortable without spending half the time worrying about potentially offending anybody. Your and your baby's comfort and well-being are paramount. Full stop. As it happened, I found carrier slings especially helpful. I have used them at home, too. They are very helpful when you need to do some housework (see Tip 12). Thanks to breastfeeding, my pre-pregnancy trousers and dresses fit me again very quickly; however, my tops did not. I forwent nursing clothes and found that a T-shirt and a button-up shirt on top worked well, as my baby could snuggle into them while feeding. The shirt on top worked like a little screen.

And another thing: you are protected by law. Always bear in mind that nobody can prevent you from breastfeeding. According to the Equality Act 2010, in England and Wales, it is classed as discrimination to treat a woman unfavourably when breastfeeding.[89] In Scotland, the law states clearly that it is a criminal offence to deny a woman the right to breastfeed, although this only applies if the child is under two years of age. Similarly, breastfeeding in public is protected by the Sex Discrimination Act 1984 in Australia and the Human Rights Act 1993 in New Zealand.[90]

Breastfeeding needs to be in the midst of our society

---

88  A. Brown, *Breastfeeding Uncovered*, Chapter 6, loc. 4253.
89  For more information see https://maternityaction.org.uk
90  http://www.legislation.gov.uk/asp/2005/1/contents

and celebrated just like eating is for adults. There is nothing disgusting or shameful about it. It is an enormous task to change opinions and attitudes, but it is not impossible. The problem is when the backup method becomes the norm, such as eating processed foods, looking up stuff on Google instead of memorising, taking the car instead of walking short distances, or throwing away items instead of repairing them.

# TIP 4

## Bedshare/Co-Sleep and Breastfeed (Breastsleep)

*Three (or more) in the bed and the little one said (most likely), "Hooray!"*

> *There is no such thing as infant sleep, there is no such thing as breastfeeding, there is only breastsleeping.*
> James McKenna and Lee Gettler[91]

In our society, we are obsessed with getting our babies to sleep through the night. We keep putting them down again, apply psychologically damaging methods such as 'controlled crying', to which a myriad of sleep-training websites bear witness. During the day, total strangers ask dreaded questions. "Is she being good?" Honest answers often produce looks ranging from surprised to critical to horrified. But what are we actually 'supposed' to do?

The NHS guidelines state that the safest place for your

---

91  https://www.ncbi.nlm.nih.gov/pubmed/26295452

baby to sleep is in a cot in your room.[92] After you have fed them (this can be their last feed at bedtime or when they wake up during the night), you are advised to place them back in their cot and not let them fall asleep on your breast.[93] My question would be, "Where else would they be going to sleep so soundly and without much of a fuss?" Falling asleep in a chair or on a sofa are all riskier and most people feeding their babies at three o'clock in the morning are bound to fall asleep there.[94] If this has been going on for about six weeks (the end of the puerperium) or more, you and the ones around you are most likely to crack. The solution? Weaning. Night weaning. Supplementing. Sleep training. But these practices all involve risks, and very often, some promising short-term results will have long-lasting negative side effects.[95]

## Is co-sleeping (breastsleeping) the answer?

When I first read about 'breastsleeping', a term coined by James McKenna and his research team, I had in effect already been doing it for about a year. Co-sleeping or breastsleeping can be seen as part of attachment parenting[96] and, just like breastfeeding, creates an amazing bond. It is

---

92  https://www.nhs.uk/conditions/pregnancy-and-baby/reducing-risk-cot-death/

93  https://www.nice.org.uk/guidance/cg37/evidence/full-guideline-addendum-485782238 and https://www.nidirect.gov.uk/conditions/sudden-infant-death-syndrome-sids

94  K. Kendall-Tackett et al., 'Mother-infant sleep locations and nighttime feeding behaviour' in *Clinical Lactation* (2010, 1, No. 1: 27–30).

95  Read the insightful passage in La Leche League, *Sweet Sleep* (2014), Chapter 18, loc. 311ff.

96  http://www.attachmentparenting.org/

what the WHO and breastfeeding experts call the 'mother-baby dyad' (two people but one person), or refer to as an 'inseparable biological and social unit'. For that is what it is. If you try and force it asunder, mother and baby (and father too) end up being broken, which in turn affects the whole of the community and ultimately humanity (see Tip 49). Sleeping and feeding are almost the same when your baby is young. They are the two primary functions which to your baby mean: *I am safe. I am loved. I am alive.*

Although it has the mother-baby dyad as its living and beating heart at its centre, co-sleeping usually involves more people – whole families, in fact – who approve of it and support it. The term 'breastsleeping', in its quirky fusion of a noun and a verb, points out one simple truth: for a baby, the breast is synonymous with food, sleep and comfort, all of which are important for their nervous system to develop and thrive. These things cannot be separated for a baby. They are of equal importance in their universe, which is as yet not fragmented by deliberation and cognitive evaluation.

Something that certainly stands in breastsleeping's favour is your baby feeling more secure and safer with you as they attune to your breathing pattern while both of you – or preferably all three of you (or more?) – are sleeping. This connection to each other's rhythms and emotions is essential, and simply not possible if your baby is napping on their own, left in a dark room in a separate cot. Co-sleeping, your body temperature will keep your baby nice and cosy.[97] It is also important that the mother is the one co-sleeping with the baby as the protection is not offered

---

97  Deborah Jackson, *Three in a Bed: The Benefits of Sleeping with Your Baby* (2003).

in the same way when sleeping with a sibling.[98]

James McKenna was able to establish that the sleep patterns of mother and baby eventually overlap nicely, night-time waking synchronises (remember your baby kicking at night while you were pregnant?),[99] and heart rate and breathing steady through direct contact.[100] Separation, meanwhile, has a physiological impact that can put the infant at risk, as their body temperature drops, their heart rate changes, stress hormones such as adrenaline and cortisol are higher, and growth hormones fall, as does the amount of proteins for normal brain function.[101] Researchers were able to record a higher rate of sleep apnoea in infants sleeping alone.[102]

It is prevalent, crucial even, for babies to continue to wake through the night.[103] Older babies manage to latch

---

98  P. S. Blair et al., CESDI SUDI Research Group, 'Babies sleeping with parents: case-control study of factors influencing the risk of the sudden infant death syndrome' in *BMJ* 1999, 319: 1457–61.

99  J. J. Mc Kenna and S. S. Mosko, 'Sleep and arousal, synchrony and independence, among mothers and infants sleeping apart and together (same bed): an experiment in evolutionary medicine' in *Acta Paediatrica* 1994, 83 (S397): 94–102.

100 B. E. Morgan et al., 'Should neonates sleep alone?' in *Biological Psychiatry* 2011, 70, No. 9: 817–25).

101 M. Reite and R. A. Short, 'Nocturnal sleep in separated monkey infants' in *Archives of General Psychiatry* 1978, Oct 1; 35 (10): 1247–53.

102 C. A. Richard, S. S. Mosko and J. J. McKenna, 'Apnea and periodic breathing in bed-sharing and solitary sleeping infants' in *Journal of Applied Physiology* (1998, Apr 1; 84 (4): 1374–80).

103 And if you are worried about your own night-time waking, consider that two stretches of sleep are physiologically healthy for humans, something Charles Dickens used to refer to as his first and second sleep, see La Leche League, *Sweet Sleep* (2014), loc. 480 and T. A Wehr et al., 'Bimodal patterns of human melatonin

themselves on very well, and you won't spend a lot of time settling them back to sleep that way.[104] In fact, I would recommend to stay away from methods such as that promoted by Tizzie Hall, who advises parents to sleep-train their babies from as early as two weeks. How can you train a helpless infant of such a tender age? Think about it. Are you actually being serious? No routines are needed at that age – they don't have one! They need round-the-clock responsive mothering, not elimination or extinction techniques or scheduled awakening. You are their comfort object and a teddy is fairly meaningless when they are that young. That will change rapidly when they metamorphose into a toddler, but why do we think we should force them to be something before they are ready? You wouldn't force yourself to go through the menopause at the age of twenty-five. Or would you?

Babies will mostly only start consolidating their sleep between six weeks and three months of age (which is the time when you are just about ready to be up and about yourself anyway).[105] It is also normal for a baby to still feed several times at night when they are over six months old. When they are about nine months old, they wake up more often again.[106] It is an almost predictable developmental

secretion consistent with a two-oscillator model of regulation' in *Neuroscience Letters*, 1995, 194 (1): 105–8.

104 https://www.saveoursleep.com/

105 S. A. Rivkees, 'Developing circadian rhythmicity in infants' in *Pediatrics* 2003, 112 (2): 373–81 and P. Peirano, C. Algarín and R. Uauy, 'Sleep-wake states and their regulatory mechanisms throughout early human development' in *Journal of Pediatrics* 2003, 143 (4): 70–9.

106 T. F. Anders, 'Night-waking in infants during the first year of life' in *Pediatrics* 1979, Jun 1; 63 (6): 860–4.

stage. Brace yourself, but take heart and remind yourself that it is only temporary. Everything is exciting as they are beginning to bottom-shuffle and learning to crawl. At this stage, a lot of parenting books recommend to 'night-wean' far too early. This has negative consequences for breastfeeding and long-term emotional health.[107]

And as another interesting side effect, toddlers who were fed at night are more independent, contrary to unfounded fears of making them dependent – the reverse is true. They make friends more quickly and are able to dress themselves at an earlier age.[108]

## What is the safest way to co-sleep, then? Or, what is the protective cuddle curl?

Of course, there are some safety guidelines to consider. Some are unfounded; others, however, should be adhered to for a good reason. Overheating has become a problem in centrally heated houses, and if you swaddle your baby, they can't move away from your body heat. Make sure that they are clothed according to the season and not smothered underneath thick blankets or duvets. They also need to sleep on a so-called 'safe surface'. A safe surface takes care of unwanted spaces between the mattress and headboard which your baby can get wedged into. You will also need to consider the softness of the mattress,[109]

---

107 A. Brown, *Breastfeeding Uncovered*, Chapter 2, loc. 1505ff. and La Leche League, *Sweet Sleep* (2014) Chapter 18, loc. 311ff.

108 M. A. Keller and W. A. Goldberg, 'Co-sleeping: Help or hindrance for young children's independence?' in *Infant and Child Development* 2004, Dec 1; 13 (5): 369–88.

109 https://www.wikihow.com/Assess-the-Safe-Firmness-of-an-Infant-Mattress-to-Prevent-Asphyxiation

sagging, unused pillows, pets, toys, heavy covers, cords, strings, and distances to the floor or sharp edges. Sofas and reclining chairs are considered unsafe surfaces as well. Now think how often you would fall asleep while forcing yourself to sit up and trying to keep yourself awake while feeding your baby. There are also fears of overlaying or suffocation under duvets and pillows, but as we will see, death by suffocation is entirely separate from SIDS. You sometimes even read about so-called 'emanations' being labelled as a risk factor for your baby, and sometimes the reverse.[110] What seems to be the risk factor here is that you are breathing out carbon dioxide, which may, in too high a concentration, affect your baby's health. However, the reverse may be true as it is this process which triggers the breathing reflex, as a higher amount of carbon dioxide makes your body want to enhance its oxygen levels, hence breathing is encouraged.[111]

Dr James McKenna considers breastfeeding as a prerequisite for bedsharing, and bedsharing a way to support breastfeeding.[112] In fact, during the early months, these cannot really be separated. Both help with the unconscious monitoring of your baby during the night

---

110 https://cosleeping.nd.edu/assets/25453/
maternal_proximity_and_infant_co2_environment_during_
bedsharing_and_possible_implications_for_sids_research.pdf
and https://scienceofmom.com/2012/07/25/new-research-on-
bedsharing-and-infant-breathing/

111 S. Mosko et al., 'Maternal proximity and infant CO2 environment during bedsharing and possible implications for SIDS research' in *American Journal of Physical Anthropology* 1997, IOS No. 3: 315–28.

112 J. J. McKenna, S. S. Mosko and C. A. Richard, 'Bedsharing promotes breastfeeding' in *Pediatrics* 1997, 100 (2): 214–19.

which is best done by adopting a sleeping position which is called "protective cuddle curl". Let your baby sleep at about the height of your breast and the crook of your arm, especially in the very early days. Hold your arm at a ninety-degree angle to protect your baby and to prevent yourself from rolling over. Lie on your side and put a pillow between your knees to be more comfortable, and rest your head on your upper arm. Just shuffle over to the other side to feed your baby on the other side. La Leche League's manual *Sweet Sleep* describes it this way: 'Your knees come up, and your arm tucks under your head or pillow, or curls around your baby, creating a protected space. There's no way for you to roll towards your baby because your bent legs won't let you. And no one else can roll into the space because your knees and elbows are in the way.' An excellent way to prevent your baby from falling out of bed is to consider buying a Next2Me cot, including an organic mattress and cover.[113]

To get a helpful overview, have a look at the UNICEF[114] guidelines for safe co-sleeping. If your baby is healthy and full-term, on their back and lightly dressed, and you are both on a safe surface, there is only a minimal risk.

---

113 For more information on this go to Tip 9, and look for Chicco cots on https://basisonline.org.uk or https://www.chicco.co.uk/chicco-products/sleeptime-and-relaxation/cribs-and-cots.html. According to research at Durham University, there is no greater risk in using these cots on postnatal wards (R. Y. Moon et al., 'SIDS and other sleep-related infant deaths: expansion of recommendations for a safe sleeping environment' in *Pediatrics* 2011, 128 (5): e1341–67.

114 https://www.unicef.org.uk/babyfriendly/news-and-research/baby-friendly-research/infant-health-research/infant-health-research-bed-sharing-infant-sleep-and-sids/

Other factors to ensure your child's (and your own) safety include being sober, a non-smoker and, you might have guessed, breastfeeding.[115] Even during sleep your baby will stay with their face near the breast because that's their first focal point where they get everything they need[116] – and it will continue to be very important and then diminish over time as they grow older.

As a bonus for yourself, you are more likely to get some restful sleep if you are breastfeeding and co-sleeping. These two cannot be separated, which is why this section on sleeping appears here rather than in the equipment section, as a baby needs their mother's body rather than a fancy crib or soother to sleep soundly. Another study found that breastfeeding and co-sleeping mothers got more sleep overall,[117] if you take into account factors such as feeding, preparing feeds and settling the baby back to sleep. (I never had to bother with any of that!)[118]

---

115 Go to the 'Safe Sleep Seven' chapter in the book *Sweet Sleep* (2014) by La Leche League, which has lots of great advice on how to prepare your sleeping space and make it safe, nursing your baby lying down on your side, sleeping styles and arrangements which vary according to personality, special needs babies or those born prematurely, and what to do when you are going back to work.

116 C. Richard et al., 'Sleeping position, orientation, and proximity in bedsharing infants and mothers' in *Sleep* 1996, 19 (9): 685–90, and H. Ball, 'Parent-infant bedsharing behavior' in *Human Nature* 2006, 17 (3): 301–18.

117 S. I. Quillin and L. L. Glenn, 'Interaction between feeding method and co-sleeping on maternal-newborn sleep' in *Journal of Obstetric, Gynecologic & Neonatal Nursing* 2004, Sep 1; 33 (5): 580–8.

118 See S. I. Quillin and L. L. Glenn above, and K. A. Kendall-Tackett, 'The effect of feeding method on sleep duration, maternal well-being, and post-partum depression' in *Clinical Lactation* 2011, 2 (2): 22–6).

It is therefore not surprising that this is what mums do – in most countries apart from those in the Western world, that is. Co-sleeping is the norm from a worldwide perspective.[119] Only in the West do we perceive babies feeding at night as something unnatural, when in fact it is the most natural thing in the world. We think it needs to be measured and reduced. Think again, and watch the brilliant video by the College of Human and Health Sciences at Swansea University.[120]

## So is this low risk compared to sleeping in a cot?

In the mid 1990s the umbrella terms 'sudden unexpected infant death' (SUID) and 'sudden unexpected death of an infant' (SUDI)[121] came into use. This phenomenon includes cases of unexplained death, accidental suffocation and strangulation in bed (ASSB), poisoning and heart problems. SIDS (Sudden Infant Death Syndrome) is only one of many factors that can lead to such a devastating and heartbreaking event or SUID/SUDI. The term ASSB is used for cases where the cause of death is known, namely suffocation or strangulation in bed. Suffocation risks have got nothing to do with SIDS. SIDS means that we don't know why the baby stopped breathing. It can be a real

---

119 H. Barry and L. M. Paxson, 'Infancy and early childhood: cross-cultural codes' in *Ethnology* 1971, 10: 466–508.

120 https://www.youtube.com/watch?v=KloS897cp-c
Instead of harmful sleep-training techniques such as controlled crying and scheduled awakening try and follow the advice on https://cosleeping.nd.edu (Dr James McKenna); http://centreforattachment.com and https://basisonline.org.uk (Dr Helen Ball, Durham University Sleep Lab).

121 https://www.gov.uk/government/news/new-guidance-aims-to-help-prevent-unexpected-child-deaths-in-london

risk for a small minority of babies with pre-existing health issues, but statistics are often lumped together and factors which can be traced back and are preventable turn up as SIDS-related data.

So, what do the statistics tell us? Ninety per cent of SIDS cases occur between one and six months of age. Occurrences peak at one to four months (seventy-five per cent of cases), when babies go through another stage of rapid cognitive development.[122] Only two per cent occur after nine months. Occurrences after one year fall outside the definition. The risk of SIDS is highest when three factors come into play:

1. Your baby is part of a vulnerable group, e.g. they were premature or a low birth weight, or have other underlying illnesses.

2. Your baby's age, as discussed above.

3. Other external factors or stressors in your baby's environment.

The four most significant external risk factors associated with SIDS are smoking,[123] lying a baby face down for

---

122 R. Y. Moon et al., 'SIDS and other sleep-related infant deaths: expansion of recommendations for a safe infant sleeping environment' in *Pediatrics* 2011, 128 (5): e1341–67).

123 K. Zhang and X. Wang, 'Maternal smoking and increased risk of sudden infant death syndrome: a meta-analysis' in *Legal Medicine* 2013, 15 (3): 115–21, and P. Fleming and P. S. Blair, 'Sudden infant death syndrome and parental smoking' in *Early Human Development* 2007, 83 (11): 721–5.

sleep,[124] leaving a baby unattended[125] and formula feeding.[126] There is also a higher risk with unvaccinated babies.[127] Interestingly, researchers were able to report the lowest rates from cultures where bedsharing is the norm.[128] Whoever would have thought?!

Formula and separate sleeping arrangements are a departure from the norm! Longer sleep at an early age is not normal! The subgroup of sober, breastfeeding, non-smoking mothers is, in fact, normal! Even as late as 2012, bedsharing was under suspicion for increasing the risk of SIDS due to the dangers of overlaying, entrapment, wedging, falling or strangulation.[129] As we have seen, none of these have anything to do with SIDS, because SIDS means that there is no known cause. All of the above are breathing hazards and easily avoided if you adhere

---

124 The "Back to Sleep" campaign was able to successfully reduce the occurrence of SIDS between 1990 and 2005 (https://pediatrics. aappublications.org/content/122/3/660?ck=nck). A baby sleeping on their tummy is a different matter on an adult's sloping chest, and can in fact be life-saving in kangaroo care for premature babies. See: N. J. Bergman and L. A. Jürisoo, 'The "kangaroo-method" for treating low birth weight babies in a developing country' in *Tropical Doctor* 1994, 24 (2): 57–60.

125 R. G. Carpenter et al., 'Sudden unexplained infant death in 20 regions in Europe: case control study' in *The Lancet* 2004, 36 (9404): 185–91.

126 F. R. Hauck et al., 'Breastfeeding and reduced risk of sudden infant death syndrome: a meta-analysis' in *Pediatrics* 2011, 128 (1): 103–10.

127 https://www.cdc.gov/vaccinesafety/concerns/sids.html and A. P. Jonville-Béra et al., 'Sudden unexpected death in infants under 3 months of age and vaccination status: a case-control study' in *British Journal of Clinical Pharmacology* 2001, 51 (3): 271–6.

128 P. Liamputtong, *Childrearing and Infant Care Issues: A Cross-Cultural Perspective* (2007).

129 See R. Y. Moon et al. above.

to the Safe Sleep Seven.[130] Scaremongering and freaking out parents will often prevent parents from giving in to a biologically normal response. The messages we receive by way of images such as billboards with axes and a headboard looking like a tombstone are meant to warn us against what is considered "bad practice"[131] but we need to realise that these are only opinions and are not based on fact. We can then just stick to common sense.

Last but not least, co-sleeping can also save you a lot of money, just like breastfeeding does: no sleep gadgets like electric rockers, apps, monitors or any other nonsense are needed to ensure your baby is monitored and safe. Guess what: you are baby's best sleep gadget, and the one they want.

Breastsleeping is a part of going green in so many ways – apart from saving resources and not supporting the cruel dairy industry by buying formula, with all its devastating environmental impacts, we are also likely to be more attached and attuned, starting with this first relationship between mother and child. A secure and loving relationship in early life is one of the foundations of a life grounded in self-respect and the respect for other people and the natural world. And once your baby has reached the toddler stage it won't only be the undiminished nutritional benefits of breastfeeding that stand in its favour. I found it was one of the best ways to calm down my toddler when she decided to throw a wobbler – when she was tired, or soaking wet after having played with watering cans in the garden and decided she did not want

---

130 http://www.uppitysciencechick.com/sleep.html
131 Dangers of Co-sleeping, Fox News broadcast (2010).

to come in; anything. It just shows you that breastfeeding is about so much more than just nutrition. It is the very foundation of all human relationships, and you may say I'm a dreamer (sorry, I stole this line from John Lennon), but I do believe the world would be a better place if more of us did what we are designed to do – nurture our babies with our bodies – and not make every effort to get them as far away from us as possible as soon as possible.

And before we move on to the next bit, here is a little afterthought. For reasons of propriety which are very much ingrained in our society, hardly anybody would think of asking you this openly, although everybody thinks it: isn't the presence of your baby in your bed going to prevent them from having any siblings? You know what I mean? (I want everyone to exchange awkward glances here.) It doesn't always have to be in your bed is all I am going to say.

# TIP 5

## Take Your Baby's Lead When Introducing Solid Food, and Buy Organic or Local Produce

*You are what you eat! 1.0*

The term 'baby-led weaning' (or BLW) has an almost mythological ring to it, as if it can be understood by only a few initiates who have access to its mysterious ways. It is definitely a lot easier than that.

To delve right into it: I would like to omit the word 'weaning'! We are not taking our babies off the breast completely as we begin to introduce solid food. The benefits of breastfeeding are undiminished, and therefore it is essential not to stop breastfeeding altogether at this stage. The central part of your baby's diet should always be breast milk before they are twelve months old. Solids are the supplement, not the other way round. Start with one feed of solids a day, which can be as little as a couple of teaspoons. Babies' stomachs are still tiny compared to yours and their digestive systems still quite immature. Gradually increase the amount of solid food after that until they can share up to three main meals and some small snacks with you during the day. Let your baby lead the way, monitor their interest in food, let them try different types of meals and experiment with textures and flavours – in other words, let them make a mess!

'Complementary feeding' or 'supplement feeding' is therefore far more appropriate to describe this process. I decided to go for a tandem approach: I tried my best to react to my daughter's cues, i.e. stopping when she indicated she had had enough, or responding to her interest if she wanted to try something – if and when it was safe enough for her to eat. Had she wanted to eat chilli or bacon rashers I certainly wouldn't have let her try too much of them. I let her feel and taste food, sometimes muck about with some of the leftovers perhaps, but still keeping an eye on her food intake. Our conditioning is, of course, that food is not for playing with, and it shouldn't be (difficult to believe in our surplus society, but here we go), but some occasional spoon-feeding and finger food worked best for me.

I firmly believe that forcing your children to eat anything they do not like is best avoided. Who won't remember aeroplanes and toys, and another spoonful for Mummy, Daddy or Granny to entice their baby or toddler to eat? I can even remember my father performing these exercises on me. You won't need to control the process as much, but you will let your baby take the lead while providing some guidance.

As for ingredients, think about fresh and locally and organically grown vegetables which are in season (there are lovely winter root vegetables which are palatable to most babies, such as parsnips), and also cereals, which have long been forgotten but used to be staples before cheap rice, pasta and potatoes flooded the market. Think of using spelt and oats, for example. Instead of ready-made baby rice, use organic rice flakes. Apart from buying the organic range at your local supermarket, try and seek out vegetable delivery schemes, or better yet, walk to a local farm if possible, or grow some veg yourself if you have the time and inclination to do so and provided you have the space to do so. But even if your space is limited, a little effort can go a long way[132]. Instead of using a food processor, just mash your baby's food up with a fork, potato masher or mixing staff.[133] Also try and buy as much Fair Trade as possible, although it is a fallacy to believe that exploitation only happens elsewhere.[134]

---

132 Find out how to grow vegetables in tubs: https://www.rhs.org.uk/advice/profile?pid=527.

133 Look at the guidelines and standards of organic farming of the Soil Association (https://www.soilassociation.org), the Marine Stewardship Council (https://www.msc.org), the Food Commission (http://www.foodcomm.org.uk) and Compassion in World Farming (https://www.ciwf.org.uk) for more information and what to look out for.

134 www.antislavery.org/

Organic food not only tastes markedly better, but there is some factual and scientifically proven evidence for its greater health benefits. According to a 2006 *Food Magazine* article, the nutritional values of our foods have been rapidly declining from 1930 to 2002 (the period of data used for the statistics). Mineral contents of calcium, iron and copper have been reduced by as much as seventy per cent.[135] A 2003 study in Atlanta taking into account a group of three- to eleven-year-old children was able to establish a significant rise in the metabolites of malathion, chlorpyriphos and pesticides in their urine samples after returning to non-organic diets.[136]

Another important distinction between the traditional way of weaning and BLW is that babies learn to swallow more solid food other than milk first when spoon-fed (due to the pureed food commonly used), and to chew first done the BLW way (as this is done mainly on non-pureed finger foods).[137] Another point is that you won't have to use ice-cube trays or end up with defrosted mush.[138] In many ways, a compromise might also be the way to go, to ensure that your baby has sufficient food intake and avoids too much spice, salt and fat. I found that spoon-feeding alongside finger foods was an excellent way to go as my baby was progressing and developing her likes and dislikes. It was more about helping her along and participating in

---

135 http://www.foodcomm.org.uk/magazines/issue_72/ (see article on: *Meat and Dairy: Where Have the Minerals Gone?*)

136 https://www.ncbi.nlm.nih.gov/pmc/articles/PMC5813803/

137 https://www.nhs.uk/news/pregnancy-and-child/spoon-feeding-compared-with-baby-led-weaning/

138 For more information see https://www.babycentre.co.uk/a1007100/baby-led-weaning

this exciting process of discovery. Being observant rather than in control prevents possible choking incidents and also allows you to introduce different types of food to your baby and gradually move on from mashed-up things to chunkier bits.

# TIP 6
## Make Your Food from Scratch

*Too many cooks spoil the broth...*

It may seem convenient to feed your baby food that has been prepared by somebody else and comes already cooked and packaged in a jar. In this respect, it is very closely related to formula feeding. But do you know how much sugar has been added, not to mention preservatives? It doesn't seem a very good idea to feed your baby overly processed foods. Just ask yourself if you would eat jarred food every day. You probably wouldn't. So why give that to your baby? Home-made baby food is relatively easy to cook and will put a lot less strain on your budget.

As soon as I gradually started to introduce solid food to my daughter's diet, I very often mashed up a few vegetables or a cooked pear, and sometimes whatever we were having with some cooking liquid, and some expressed breast milk so she could handle it. Other good candidates are sweet potato, carrots, peas and apples. Instead of pureeing everything, which is generally only necessary if you start weaning before six months (which isn't recommended by the WHO),[139] you can then mash, press through a sieve, steam, boil or let the baby reach out for whatever they fancy – with necessary caution, of course.

I found that using grains such as rice flakes, oats or spelt, and starchy vegetables, as a base worked very well, and then adding veggies or fruit. That way, I made sure my daughter had her share of grains, fibre, protein and vitamins as a supplement to my breast milk, and had hence eaten a complete meal. I let her join in when we were having soup, while being careful not to add salt or any other seasoning. Sometimes I took a portion out of the pan before I continued with the cooking for my husband and myself. After a while, when your baby is ready, think about adding a bit of meat (up to 25 g) to the above. If you are vegetarian or vegan, there is lots of advice available to make sure your baby gets all they need.[140] You can also use rice, spelt or maize cakes with a bit of water or milk and banana for a quick meal if you are pressed for time (which we all are sometimes).

# RECIPES

## Cooked pear

Wash, quarter, core and peel the pear (eat some slices yourself). Cut about one quarter of it into small cubes and put into a small pan, just covered with water, and bring to a boil. Add 2 tbsp of porridge oats or rice flakes if you like, stir well, add more water if needed and mash the bits

---

139 https://kellymom.com/ages/older-infant/delay-solids/
140 https://www.nhs.uk/conditions/pregnancy-and-baby/vegetarian-vegan-children/

of fruit so your baby can handle it. This recipe also works well with bits of banana.

## Potatoes and carrot

Wash and peel the potato and carrot and cut them into small cubes. A small potato and about half a medium carrot are generally enough when you're starting out with solids. Cook until soft and leave a bit of the cooking water to mash or puree it. If your baby is over six months old, mashing it up is generally enough.

## Hokkaido pumpkin and sweet potato

Wash, peel and cube the pumpkin and sweet potato. About a handful of each is usually enough. Cover with water and bring to a boil. Turn down the heat and cook until soft, then mash it up.

Add some variation by replacing the pumpkin with courgettes, standard potatoes or parsnips according to season.

# TIP 7

## Get a Safe-to-Use Sippy Cup and Use Alternatives to Plastic Food Storage Containers and Cutlery

*Splashy drumsticks!*

As soon as your baby can sit in a high chair and can handle pureed or mashed-up food, it is time to introduce a sippy cup. Preferably, it should also be a free-flow cup without a valve inserted, as the current recommendation is that babies should learn to drink from a cup and not suck the liquid from a sippy top as they would from a bottle or the breast .[141]

Inevitably, most products on the market are made from plastic. It does make sense in this case, as the cup will end up on the floor and be used as a drumstick on the high chair's table more often than not. If your baby refuses to use a sippy cup like mine did, at least initially, try and help them drink from the cup without a top, even if they start by lapping it up like a kitten. They'll learn how to do it after a while. Eventually, my daughter was happy to use the Munchkin sippy cup without a spout, which is, I am pleased to say, BPA free.[142] Stainless steel and glass are good alternatives too.[143] At this stage, you might also want to invest in some plates and spoons made from plastic-free materials.[144] Another idea is to recycle small glass yoghurt

---

141 https://www.babycenter.com/0_sippy-cup-dos-and-donts_1439508. bc and http://www.child-smile.org.uk/parents-and-carers/birth-to-3-years-old/drinking-from-a-cup.aspx

142 https://www.munchkin.co.uk/cups/spoutless-cups.html

143 https://gimmethegoodstuff.org/safe-product-guides/sippy-cups/ Look for the CE logo and BS EN 14350 for drinking equipment, and BS EN 1400 for soothers (https://shop.bsigroup.com/).

144 Look on websites such as https://nmcommunity.uk/ or https://babipur.co.uk

If you are looking for some inspiration to make your recipes more interesting, https://www.kitchenstewardship.com is another great resource, and also for when your kids grow older. Ask at your local library for some cookbooks such as L. Barnes's *Cooking for Baby*, which is a more traditional approach. Look on https://ecolunchboxes.com or https://www.anythingbutplastic.co.uk for a stainless-steel box.

jars and sterilise them in a low oven or with boiling water. I did the same thing with bamboo feeding spoons. I stopped doing it after a month or two and gave my baby filtered tap water to drink and used clean glass jars and bamboo spoons, which are also dishwasher safe. Bamboo plates are a good alternative. It is also worth investing in some reusable and BPA-free lunch boxes.

## The problem with BPA

We are now very much aware of phthalates in products made from plastics and the risks associated with them.[145] Bisphenol A (or BPA for short) is thought to have oestrogenic properties and may even be one of the reasons why sperm counts have plummeted in the last couple of decades.[146] BPA in particular has also been linked to ADHD and diabetes as well as some types of cancer.[147]

Unfortunately, just going for the BPA-free products is often not good enough. Bisphenol S (BPS), another component of plastic-based products very similar to BPA, might be just as harmful as an endocrine disruptor.[148] BPA is one of the main ingredients for the manufacturing of polycarbonate (PC), and BPS is an organic chemical used to make polysulfone.[149] Food

---

145 Go to Tip 16 for more information on this.

146 https://www.gq.com/story/sperm-count-zero

147 For more research on BPA see https://www.nhs.uk/news/
pregnancy-and-child/questions-raised-over-bpa-plastic/

148 https://www.scientificamerican.com/article/bpa-free-plastic-
containers-may-be-just-as-hazardous/

149 https://www.sciencedirect.com/topics/chemical-engineering/
polysulfones

packaging, plastic utensils and baby bottles are just a few examples of products made with PC, whereas the primary usage of BPS is in thermal papers (the stuff used for receipts) and inks. Bisphenol F (BPF),[150] another member of the bisphenol family, has been detected in many everyday products, such as personal care products (e.g. body wash, haircare products, make-up, lotions and toothpaste), paper products (e.g. currency, flyers, tickets, mailing envelopes and aeroplane boarding passes) and food (e.g. dairy products, meat and meat products, vegetables, canned foods, and cereals). That is pretty much everything wrapped in plastic.[151] Some of the research is not entirely conclusive, but for as long as we don't know for sure it is best to opt for other product ranges.[152] A recent study by a team at the Korea Institute of Toxicology[153] tested zebrafish embryos and larvae to find evidence for the effect of BPS and BPF in their thyroid function. They were able to establish that BPS and BPF are directly related to increased thyroid hormone levels. This finding will increase concerns about the growing trend of manufacturers substituting BPA in their products for these compounds, which

---

150 BPF is used to make epoxy resins and coatings, especially for systems requiring increased thickness and durability, such as tank and pipe linings, industrial floors, road and bridge deck toppings, structural adhesives, grouts, coatings and electrical varnishes (https://www.scientificamerican.com/article/bpa-free-plastic-containers-may-be-just-as-hazardous/).

151 http://time.com/3742871/bpa-free-health/ and https://ehp.niehs.nih.gov/doi/10.1289/ehp.1408989

152 https://ntp.niehs.nih.gov/results/areas/bpa/index.html

153 https://chemicalwatch.com/73251/south-korean-study-bps-bpf-disrupt-zebrafish-thyroid-function

are structurally similar at the molecular level but are much less well understood in terms of toxicity. The Consortium Linking Academic and Regulatory Insights on BPA Toxicity Program (CLARITY-BPA)[154] was a two-year guideline-compliant study of potential BPA toxicity in rats. It looked at the effects on all parts of the nervous and endocrine systems as well as the reproductive organs (testes or ovaries). The results of the study have shown that BPA has an impact on fetal development, although not all parts of the body are affected in the same way. In some cases the effects are only transient; in others, they are likely to be longer-lasting. There is also some evidence that these chemicals make their way into our food.[155] It should therefore now be regarded as common sense not to microwave your food in plastic containers, but that is unfortunately not the only thing to look out for, as the plastic bags in which we store our cereals are likely to shed some minute particles of plastic which we then involuntarily ingest.[156] Luckily, however, these compounds do not seem to hang about in our bodies for too long, as a 2011 study[157] was able to establish. Eating home-cooked food and avoiding plastic packaging whenever possible for just a short amount of time resulted in significantly lower levels of BPA and the phthalate DEHP[158] in the participants' urine samples.

---

154 https://ntp.niehs.nih.gov/results/areas/bpa/index.html
155 https://www.ncbi.nlm.nih.gov/pubmed/22889897
156 https://learn.eartheasy.com/articles/is-food-packaging-safe/
157 https://silentspring.org/detox-me-app-tips-healthier-living
158 https://www.hindawi.com/journals/bmri/2018/1750368/

# TIP 8

## Be Aware of Your Diet – and Do Something About It

*You are what you eat. 2.0*

After the long months of pregnancy and abstaining from some of your favourite foods, you probably can't wait for a treat. This is going to continue to some degree for as long as you are breastfeeding. But even if you are planning to wean before the recommended two years, this is an opportune time to give your diet an overhaul and not relapse into 'bad' habits.

As long as you are breastfeeding the connection between what you feed yourself and what your baby is receiving is still very direct, which is why alcohol is banned and caffeine limited to a minimum, preferably not more than two cups of a caffeinated beverage a day. Remember that green tea contains caffeine. Rooibos or Honeybush teas are very good alternatives.[159] Beware of vegetables such as broccoli, cabbage and dairy products, especially cow's milk. It is now considered to be unproblematic to eat peanuts unless there is a propensity to allergies in your family. In order to find out if anything you have eaten may have caused irritability, tummy upsets or nappy rash, try and remember what it was, watch your baby closely and see if the same thing happens again the next time you eat a certain type of food.

Start sourcing organic and preferably local produce, and think twice before buying on the cheap. I find it somewhat bewildering that it is widely regarded as OK to go cheap with food, but items like prams can be

---

159 Try Dragonfly tea (https://dragonflytea.com/) for some lovely flavours.

expensive. You may also want to include a suitable dietary supplement, such as Wild Nutrition,[160] and herbal teas. Fennel and camomile are safe to drink.[161] You may want to consider seeking out a medical herbalist[162] in your area and asking them for herbal breastfeeding tea or a prescription to support your breastfeeding and overall health. By the time my daughter was eighteen months old, I had begun to feel quite tired, and herbal tinctures have helped me a great deal to feel well within myself.

Try and use different grains as staples in your diet – perhaps a spelt and pesto risotto instead of one made with Arborio rice, oats for crumble toppings, or pearl barley in soup. These are good alternatives to rice and pasta. Stay seasonal with your vegetables as much as you can. When you shop at the big supermarkets, buy UK produce; with some notable exceptions – nothing is wrong with a banana, but do go for Rainforest Alliance/Fair Trade. And save them for a special treat. Meat should also be treated as something special. What about consuming it only once or twice a week?[163] Remember that you are already setting an example to your child and cut down on sugary drinks as well as your general sugar consumption. It is gratifying to bake and cook your own things. Invest in a few easy-to-follow and traditional cookbooks or browse on the web,[164] and enjoy your home cooking.

---

160 https://www.wildnutrition.com; see Tip 21 for more information.
161 Dragonfly tea (https://dragonflytea.com) has a lovely range of flavoured rooibos teas. Their teabags are also plastic free. Teapigs (https://www.teapigs.co.uk/) also use plastic-free teabags and have delicious herbal mixes.
162 https://www.nimh.org.uk/
163 Learn more here: https://www.meatfreemondays.com/
164 https://www.kitchenstewardship.com/

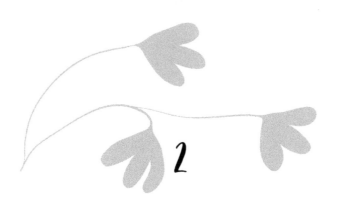

# Fashion Statements and
# Baby Equipment Anxiety

*The emperor marched in the procession under the
beautiful canopy, and all who saw him in the street and out
of the windows exclaimed: "Indeed, the emperor's new suit
is incomparable! What a long train he has! How well it fits
him!" Nobody wished to let others know he saw nothing, for
then he would have been unfit for his office or too stupid.
Never emperor's clothes were more admired.*

*"But he has nothing on at all," said a little child at last.
"Good heavens! Listen to the voice of an innocent child," said
the father, and one whispered to the other what the child had
said. "But he has nothing on at all," cried, at last, the whole
people. That made a deep impression upon the emperor, for it
seemed to him that they were right; but he thought to himself,
"Now I must bear up to the end." And the chamberlains
walked with still greater dignity as if they carried the train
which did not exist.*

'The Emperor's New Suit' in
*Delphi Complete Works of Hans Christian Andersen*

## Conspicuous consumption

As we can see from Hans Christian Andersen's well-known tale, it is dependent on social conventions and expectations what we think we need and what we choose to buy to impress. And impressing people can become more important than what we need. The item itself means nothing, is in fact null and void, apart from its function as a means of a display of power. Mothering your baby in a caring, down-to-earth way can become inundated and obliterated by gadgets and items that will ultimately gather dust. Too much stuff won't be very good for the environment either, as resources have been used to produce all of these items, a lot of which are hardly ever used or not at all, and then end up in landfill or at best passed around or in charity shops. But why do we feel an almost compulsive need to do this? Conspiracy theories aside, it seems to be a very human trait to succumb to these methods of display.

The phenomenon of feasting and the material display of wealth are quite possibly as old as the human race, and are also known as conspicuous consumption, a term first introduced by the Norwegian economist Thorstein Veblen in 1899.[165] It refers to the distinctive behaviour of buying expensive items as a means to display our social status rather than to serve our actual needs. And it does make sense – the wealthier we are, the more money we have to spare for things that go beyond our mere subsistence level. But even though Veblen mainly had the Industrial Revolution in mind, and the large-scale production of goods that went along with it, equating material wealth

---

165 http://moglen.law.columbia.edu/LCS/theoryleisureclass.pdf

with political power or perhaps even spiritual influence is nothing new – we need it as a substitute to demonstrate our wielding of intangible forces. Power. Influence. Might.

In pre-industrial civilisations the feasting still had a spiritual component attached to it. Examples of these practices were common amongst the Haida, a people of British Columbia.[166] There was always something more in the performing of these rites, something that put the community in touch with their ancestors from the past and also reached out into the future. Thereby, a chief established his position by mystically displaying his material wealth.

## But how did we get to a stage where we own so much and value so little?

The economy relies on people needing new things or suggesting that they do to grow. And yet, there is ample proof that this model has become very much obsolete. Or, as George Monbiot put it, this is 'the impossibility of growth'.[167]

The main problem, as I see it, is being conned into always buying more than we require and misinterpreting this behaviour as our genuine need. We do not only live in a materialist culture – it is also a throwaway culture. Throwing 'stuff' away is part of the process, such as too much food, too much packaging and, quite frankly, items that are deliberately not made to last, such as a lot of

---

166 https://www.thediscourse.ca/reconciliation/made-haida-clan-potlatch-historic
167 https://www.monbiot.com/2014/05/27/the-impossibility-of-growth/

children's toys. If you can afford to buy things and not care about them very much at all, is often treated as a measure of success.

So, before we binge-buy, perhaps we should consider a few facts and then decide if we want to go along with the spree or if we could perhaps consume a little bit less. Two toys can become more meaningful and therefore more valuable if your child hasn't got another fifteen to distract them.

# TIP 9
## Only Buy What You Need When You Need It, and Buy a Lot of Items Second-Hand

*Wait a minute, what about the nursery?*

Welcome to the glittering world of baby gear and fully kitted out nurseries, including gadgets you have never heard of before. Specially designed feeding pillows, teething pads for baby carriers (these are useful, I admit), electric warmers for baby wipes, electric baby rockers, swaddling blankets, baby monitors, sleep apps and baby hammocks.[168] But what do you *really* need?

Apart from being fed, and kept warm or cool with appropriate clothing, your baby needs somewhere safe and clean to sleep, and a safe way to make journeys and to be carried inside and outside the house. And that is it.

---

168 It is quite puzzling how humanity was able to thrive without all that nonsense. Read a discussion of these items in La Leche League's *Sweet Sleep* (2014), Chapter 12 (see Recommended Reading).

And yet, the nursery and all its equipment feature centre stage in most parenting books, but this can all come later. A cot is both useful for daytime naps and then, at some point, when your baby does move into their own bed. For that stage, appropriate bedding is a concern, which I will discuss below.

Perhaps it has something to do with conspicuous consumption, nest-building or just a feeling that this is a way to show how welcome your new, tiny human being is, and how eagerly you have been awaiting their arrival. I found myself going frantic with wanting to set up a nursing corner with a rocking chair and a footstool, only to find out afterwards that I would feed my daughter anywhere around the house (and on the go) whenever she indicated that she needed a feed. If you think about what babies need, it isn't a separate room, and certainly not before they are six months or even a year old. The recommendation is to let them sleep with you in the same room for at least the first six months; better even for the whole of the first year (go back to Tip 4 for more information).

So a beautifully decorated nursery is mainly something parents do for themselves, to comply with their relatives (think of overzealous grandparents) or to impress their friends. If, however, preparing a room for your baby is still something you absolutely think is essential and you want to start decorating before your baby is even born, think about the potential hazards lurking in the paints, varnishes and glues we use for our interiors. The following information is, of course, also valid if you decide to do it a little later and your baby has grown into a toddler.

It is definitely a better idea to go for eco paints, which use traditional ingredients such as chalk, kaolin and natural oils such as linseed and eucalyptus to avoid exposure to VOCs and chemicals. And while you are decorating, think about investing in a fume absorber/air purifier.[169] Generally, wooden floorboards are preferable to carpeting or vinyl. Look for FSC/PEFC certified[170] ones if you need new ones. An alternative is to use carpeting made from natural fibres, and this also applies to rugs and curtains.

Another thing to think about is the exposure to electromagnetic fields (EMFs), which has increased immeasurably within the last few decades due to our

---

169 https://www.healthy-house.co.uk has a great range of air purifiers/ fume absorbers and hypoallergenic bedding, as well as toiletries.

170 The Forest Stewardship Council (FSC) is a global certification system to identify and purchase wood from well-managed forests. It defines ten principles of responsible forest management. The Programme for the Endorsement of Forest Certification (PEFC) describes itself as an international organisation dedicated to promoting sustainable forest management (SFM) through independent third-party certification. However, PEFC is not a standards agency but a mutual recognition scheme. It not only focuses on the ethical aspects of SFM, but also the processing of timber, resulting in a greater emphasis on the supply chain than FSC offers. While both are committed to the same cause, the primary difference between the certifications is their origins. Initially, the FSC scheme was developed for tropical environments and not suited to forests in Europe and North America. This led to the introduction of PEFC in the late 1990s, to facilitate SFM certification in Europe. PEFC now accounts for over 264 million hectares of certified forests and its certification system is recognised in over thirty countries. Meanwhile, FSC has certified forests in over eighty countries, with seven per cent of the world's forest area (180 million hectares) carrying the FSC certification. GfK (https://www.gfk.com/) data collected in 2014 showed that fifty per cent of people in the UK recognise the FSC logo (https://fsc.org/en/news/half-uk-public-recognise-fsc-sustainable-forests-logo).

usage of home computers and mobile phones. The effect of electronic devices on our health is not yet entirely clear as a lot of exposure is rather recent so we don't have any evidence as to the long-term effects. What we do know, however, is that there has been an increase in depression, irritability, headaches, migraines and hypersensitivity due to overuse of computers, TVs, mobile phones, and the instalment of mobile phone masts in the vicinity of our homes. It is, therefore, a good idea to remove these sources of stimulation from your own and your child's bedroom as much as possible, as they can lead to a disruption in sleeping patterns.

# NATURAL SLEEPY-TIME EQUIPMENT

## *Cots*

When it comes to somewhere to sleep other than in the parent's bed, there are different options to choose from, such as Moses baskets and cribs for the very early days and weeks, and cots, cot-beds and Next2Me cots for later.[171] It is undoubtedly a more economical solution to buy a cot-bed, although you are bound to play 'I Spy' with your tiny newborn in it, but at least you will have a bed you will be able to use for quite a long time. A lot of people start with a bassinet or crib, although babies are likely to outgrow these before they are six months old.

Another ecological and economical solution is to buy a cot that will last from day one to the toddler stage, such

---

171 Make sure they comply with safety standards when choosing one, and look for BS EN 716 and BS EN 716-1-1996 on the label (see https://www.bsigroup.com/ for respective standard coding).

as the Mokee cot.[172] This is simple in its design, and the manufacturers use certified wood.[173] And it doesn't cost the earth. You can add a natural mattress for an additional cost and both of them together will cost you £150 at the time of writing (2018). With the Mokee cot, you can also avoid investing in a custom-made changing unit as it comes with a changing station accessory for very little extra cost.[174]

If you are comfortable with second-hand, look for things on Facebook's marketplace. Very often, there are gently used cots available. As always when buying things second-hand, have a good look at the item before you commit, and make sure everything is included (including instruction booklets). Supporting your local charity shops is another good alternative. And find out what you can reuse and recycle yourself.[175] Buying or otherwise acquiring gently used items is not only good for your wallet, but also reduces the pollution caused by making new products – which will only end up in landfill.

---

172 https://en.mokee.eu/cot.html

173 While on the lookout for sustainable wood, consider FSC (https://www.fsc-uk.org) and PEFC (https://pefc.org) approved wood, and avoid medium-density fibreboard (MDF) as this contains glue that binds together the wood chips, and is a health hazard as small particles and formaldehyde can be breathed in and enter the lungs.

174 https://en.mokee.eu/collections/cot-accessories/products/pokee?variant=

175 When you want to sell products or pass on items it is a good idea to check on the Child Accident Prevention Trust website (https://www.capt.org.uk/) for updates and guidelines. The Baby Products Association (http://www.b-p-a.org/bpa-org/home.asp) is another important resource.

## *Mattresses*

Unlike the cot, the mattress should not be bought second-hand. There is a risk of used mattresses harbouring bacteria such as *Staphylococcus aureus*, which is another potential cause of SIDS.[176] The Lullaby Trust[177] regularly update their recommendations, so it is well worth having a look on their website.

Mattresses need to be firm and fit the crib, cot or cot-bed properly.[178] In 1992, a study on SIDS was published which indicated a significant correlation between babies sleeping on their tummies and infant death.[179] The National Cot Death Prevention Programme in New Zealand, which has been going on since 1994, has had very high success rates. Due to the dedicated work of midwives and other healthcare professionals, parents have been shown how to wrap their babies' mattresses correctly. Amongst the over two hundred thousand New Zealand babies sleeping on mattresses with specially formulated polyethylene covers, not a single case of SIDS has occurred.[180]

Eco mattresses[181] are made from different materials such as coir or coconut fibre, lamb's or sheep wool, mohair

---

176 https://www.ncbi.nlm.nih.gov/books/NBK513388/

177 https://www.lullabytrust.org.uk/

178 See Tip 9.

179 https://pediatrics.aappublications.org/content/105/3/650; see also the updated evidence base by The Lullaby Trust: https://www.lullabytrust.org.uk/wp-content/uploads/Evidence-base-2019.pdf.

180 https://www.healthychild.com/has-the-cause-of-crib-death-sids-been-found/

181 Baby Products Association guidelines are to leave no more than 4 cm between the edge of the mattress and the edge of the cot. Cot mattresses should be labelled with BS 1877 and BS 7177.

or natural latex (see below). They all have their pros and cons, and which of them you ultimately choose is mostly a matter of personal preference.

The problem with conventional wool used to be so-called sheep-dipping. Farmers commonly used a bath of organophosphates, which are thought to cause chronic illnesses such as chronic fatigue syndrome.[182] It is important to note, however, that this used to be common practice in the 1970s, 1980s and 1990s. Farmers now tend to use other sheep dip treatments to minimise the consumers' risk of exposure to the chemicals.[183]

Polybrominated diphenyl ethers (PBDEs) used as fire-retardant chemicals in mattresses may affect thyroid and brain development and can cause cancer, as shown in laboratory mice. These can even cross the placenta and find their way into breast milk.[184]

Latex can be linked to asthma and skin allergies,[185] while polyvinyl chloride (PVC), often used as a seal on the outside of mattresses, has been linked to cancer, congenital disabilities, genetic changes, chronic bronchitis, ulcers, skin diseases, deafness, vision failure, indigestion and liver dysfunction.[186] Polyurethane foam, which is also often

182 https://www.meassociation.org.uk/2015/06/organophosphate-sheep-dipping-short-commons-debate-10-june-2015/
183 https://www.sepa.org.uk/media/123372/sheep_dipping_code_of_practice.pdf
184 https://www.nrdc.org/experts/kristi-pullen/identifying-endocrine-disrupting-chemicals-using-toxcast-and-authoritative; https://www.ncbi.nlm.nih.gov/pmc/articles/PMC2612591/ and https://www.ncbi.nlm.nih.gov/pmc/articles/PMC5266592/
185 http://www.hse.gov.uk/healthservices/latex/
186 http://www.chej.org/pvcfactsheets/PVC_Policies_Around_The_World.html

used in mattresses, can harbour bacteria and is difficult to clean. Generally, try and avoid human-made fibres such as bleached or peroxide-treated materials, nylon, polyester, polyester-cotton mixes, and fleeces.

Whenever possible, try and buy locally to reduce transport miles and support local businesses.[187] Retailers and manufacturers such as Herdysleep[188] and the Natural Bed Company[189] sell mattresses (bespoke if needed), pillows, duvets and even woollen beds handmade in Britain from British wool. Herdysleep even make an effort to cut down on waste by vacuum-packaging their mattresses. That way, you will also get them up the stairs and through doors more easily. You can also purchase an organic cotton pillow and mattress protector. These are worthwhile investments as this is a good time to stop sleeping on a chemical cocktail yourself. Herdysleep also make sure that most of their packaging is recyclable. For mattresses to fit specific cots and cribs, try The Little Green Sheep[190] or Naturalmat.[191] The Little Green Sheep has mattresses available that fit standard cots and cot-beds. The ingenious idea of making them firmer on one side will allow you to switch from the firmer support needed for babies up to about twelve months to a more toddler- and preschool-age-appropriate mattress.

Table 4 below is an overview of the natural fibres used for babies' mattresses, including their specific benefits.

---

187 Try companies like Woolroom, Herdysleep, Greenfibres, the Natural Bed Company and Cottonsafe (see the Resources Directory at the end of this book).

188 https://www.herdysleep.com/

189 https://www.naturalbedcompany.co.uk/

190 https://www.thelittlegreensheep.co.uk/

191 https://www.naturalmat.co.uk/

| TYPE OF MATTRESS | BENEFITS |
|---|---|
| Coir, Coco-Mat or coconut fibre.[192] | Elastic and orthosomatic (i.e. adapts to your body shape/form). |
| Lambswool/sheep wool.[193] | Resistant to dust mites. Thermal insulator (i.e. cosy in winter and cool in summer) Flame-retardant properties. Orthosomatic. |
| Mohair (from the angora goat).[194] | Excellent temperature regulator. Light. Soft. Breathable. |
| Natural latex.[195] | Made from the sap of rubber tree, therefore environmentally friendly, breathable and elastic. |

Table 4: *Natural Mattresses*

## *Bedding*

Generally, there shouldn't be any pillows or thick duvets in your baby's bed or sleeping place to avoid overheating or suffocation. Best are flat sheets or fitted sheets, cellular blankets and sleeping bags.[196] You can get them in different

---

192 https://www.coco-mat.com/int_en/

193 https://www.herdysleep.com/

194 https://www.heals.com/natural-sleep-mohair-mattress.html

195 https://www.latexsense.co.uk/

196 Look for 2.5 tog (suitable for a room temperature from 10–20 °C), so you can use it all year round, although the room temperature should preferably be about 21 °C. Sleeping bags are ideal for babies who tend to kick off their covers. A zipper makes it easy to change the nappy during the night. They are intended for use without additional bedding, so never use a sleeping bag with a duvet, and ensure yours conforms to BS 8510:2009. Make sure

togs, and check beforehand which one to use at what room temperature. It is generally recommended that your baby should sleep in a room at about 18 °C (65 °F).[197]

# Are we there yet?
## *The inevitable car seat and pram*

Ask yourself, hand on heart, if you really need the £1,000 pram. And do you need to spend hours on end researching the best travel system? It's also an idea not to be blinded by the newest model. Its main new feature may only be a different pattern on the cover. And is it going to do the job so much better than the 'old model', which, let's face it, was perfectly fine for parents whose babies have reached the ripe old age of six months?

To keep costs a little bit lower, try and invest in a three-part travel system. They are relatively expensive upfront when bought new, but you will save money by not having to buy a car seat, a pram and a pushchair separately. They are also quite easy to use as a carrycot which is suitable for babies of up to six months in age, a car seat which also clicks into the chassis, and later as a pushchair seat which you can use from six months. A complete travel system also comes with a click-in base for the car.

We found a brilliant Britax[198] three-part travel system in a charity shop, just as the previous owner was about to donate it, who was somebody we knew. It was more like the

---

you get the right size so your baby's head cannot slip inside the sleeping bag when they are in it.

197 https://www.sth.nhs.uk/clientfiles/File/Sleep%20Safe%20 inners%20[web][1].pdf

198 https://www.britax-roemer.co.uk/

luck of the draw, but I wouldn't recommend it if you are not sure what has happened to it previously. Another advantage of buying second-hand is that very often these items have been aired enough so that the chemicals used during the manufacturing process have evaporated sufficiently. For the first few months, I found myself happily using just the baby carriers/slings and sometimes clipping the car seat into the chassis. I never actually used the pram or carrycot, which is why it makes sense to think about where you live and how you are going to run your day-to-day errands.

If your car boot is small, you might want to get an umbrella-folding buggy, which you can use from six months.[199] If you are into the outdoors, consider an all-terrain pram (ATP)[200] with large wheels that glide over bumps and can be pushed in front of you while you are exercising or perhaps taking your older baby or toddler to outdoor parent-and-toddler groups.

| CAR SEAT STAGE | WEIGHT RANGE | AGE RANGE |
|---|---|---|
| 0 | 0–10 kg (22 lbs) | Birth – about 6–9 months |
| 0+ | 0–13 kg (29 lbs) | Birth – about 12–15 months |
| 1 | 9–18 kg (20–40 lbs) | 9 months – 4 years |
| 2 | 15–25 kg (33–55 lbs) | 4–7 years |
| 3 | 22–36 kg (48–79 lbs) and 125 cm or taller | 4–11 years |

Table 5: *Car Seat Stages and their Respective Weight and Age Ranges*
Source: https://www.childcarseats.org.uk/types-of-seat/

199 http://www.quinny.com/gb-en/
200 https://www.madeformums.com/reviews/10-of-the-best-all-terrain-and-3-wheeler-buggies/

By the time your baby is about eight to nine months old, they will have outgrown the car seat that came with the complete travel system. This, unfortunately, means that you will be out looking for another one. There is no way around it: if you are travelling in the car, your baby has to be in a correctly installed car seat, and for a very good reason.[201] In this case, the advice to buy a new one probably isn't just the callousness of manufacturers. You have to make sure the car seat is undamaged and complete in order for it to function correctly. It's safest to have your baby travel facing backwards on the back seat. If you have them travelling next to you on the passenger front seat, make sure you have deactivated the airbag. The law is currently changing, and it won't be considered safe enough to let your baby or child travel facing the front any longer if they weigh less than 18 kg. According to the advice on the Joie website, 'children should ride rearward facing until at least 15 months. Many global safety experts recommend continuing past 15 months, up to two years, three years or even up to 4 years as required in Sweden'.[202] According to 2015 internal ECE testing with Q.1.5 dummies who were placed in the seats rearward facing sustained seventy-three per cent less tension in the neck in case of a frontal impact during the test runs.[203] The seat will absorb most of the impact when facing backwards

---

201 For more in-depth information visit https://www.childcarseats. org.uk

202 https://www.joiebaby.com/lookbacklonger/

203 For more information see Footnote 81. A new range of car seats come with a base, as it is deemed unsafe to secure your child's car seat with just the belt. Do have a good look and ask trained staff in store before you commit.

and the child's head, neck and spine are much better protected.

The car seat stages given above are only a rough guide. There are also a lot of combination seats available, and it is best to seek expert advice before you commit.

## *But how can I keep an eye on them?*

Keeping an eye on a tiny baby while getting on with household chores, preparing meals or giving older siblings your attention can be a real challenge. A lot of it can be resolved by carrying your baby snugly and securely in a sling, which is relatively easy to do for the first six months. That also makes overuse of the playpen obsolete.[204] I found it helpful to swap places. Sometimes my baby was quite happy in her bouncy chair, which I used until she was about four months. It became unsafe when she started to become very mobile and began to wriggle out. For short periods of time she was happy on her play mat, then I put her back in the sling. We only ever used the big playpen when she got to the crawling stage and then only for very short amounts of time, for example when I needed the loo or had to pack bags to get ready to go out. Mostly, I carried her on my back while I was doing household chores, or let her sleep in her Moses basket while I was in the kitchen or writing this book. Sometimes she would feed on my lap and fall asleep while doing so, or happily sit on my

---

204 Initially I was absolutely against it, but then I did see some of its benefits – at least occasionally. As long as my daughter was happy enough it was helpful (especially when she got really mobile from about seven to eight months onwards), for example if I just wanted to nip to the toilet.

lap. And then I had to interrupt whatever I was doing, but then I would sometimes get an hour or so while her daddy was looking after her. It was my attempt at treating my child as part of my life and not as an adjunct or satellite that needed to be fitted around my old life. I found she was happiest while being allowed to participate rather than being amused with toys and then left again. It just seemed to be what made her happy. And then I started to let her roam free as much as I could. The idea is to involve children right from the start. You can give them some dry laundry to play with while you fold up the rest to be put away in the cupboard, for example.

While this is all about involving them in what you do during the day, getting them off to sleep at night is another challenge. And then what? Leave them? Then listen out, hoping they won't wake up yet again, and then start the whole cycle again? Chances are, they still want to be involved. Here's an idea: why not try and establish a bedtime routine which involves you and your baby together rather than going through a long, drawn-out struggle trying to put them down in their cot, picking them up and going through all of it time and time again until both of you (and your partner) are entirely worn out? Why not let your baby fall asleep next to you, preferably while being fed, or let them sleep soundly in a cot or on a duvet in the living room, while you spend some time with hubby and then go to sleep yourself? Chances are you'll need it. And all of this works without baby monitors. These devices are just yet more pieces of equipment which produce more electronic waves with potentially adverse effects.[205]

---

205 https://www.home-biology.com/electromagnetic-radiation/high-

Although a bedtime routine as described above may not work for you (because everyone is different and so is every baby), it is just an idea to perhaps make things easier for everybody.

## *Splish, splash, we are taking a bath*

Bath time is one of those special moments of the day for your baby to enjoy. They can enjoy some nappy-free time and splash about in the water. It is also a good starting point for a bedtime routine. Unlike most of the other items, a baby bath undoubtedly has fewer issues when bought second-hand. It is not an absolute essential, but I found it very useful for the first few baths. As soon as they can sit up by themselves securely, you can also use it for special playtime with buckets, sponges and bath books, placing it in the big tub or shower.[206] You might even consider using a washing-up bowl for the first gentle introduction to a nice and hopefully relaxing bath time experience. The first couple of times, my little one almost screamed the place down. Perhaps it was my ineptitude as a new mum, or maybe it was just too cold and uncomfortable – who knows?

However, we got into the swing of it pretty quickly. As she got older, we just hopped in with her, either in the big bath or under the shower. Take care if you are nervous about this. For my part, I found it worked perfectly well for us. Keep a good grip on your baby, though, as of course they can be very slippery once wet

---

frequency-electromagnetic-fields/monitors-radiation

206 For bath toys go to Chapter 7. For healthy and silicone-, SLS- and palm-oil-free bath time ideas, see Tip 16.

and all the wrigglier as they grow older. Introduce your baby to the water gently and look up tips on bathing[207] for the early months and how to make sure your baby is safe. You will see if your baby is happy letting the water run down the back of their head. Leaflets given out by the NHS are often helpful in this regard as they include lots of advice and ideas.

## A dressing table for your baby

Before you rush into anything, consider whether another piece of furniture might work just as well. Otherwise, a changing station is just another item of clutter that can't even be upcycled for much else. Why not make do without one altogether? To me, changing my daughter on a changing mat on the floor was the best solution, simply because she couldn't roll off any precipitous heights. Sometimes, I even changed her on my lap like they used to in the old days. I kept another mat in the bedroom, so I wouldn't have to walk downstairs if I needed to change a nappy during the night. As soon as we started to introduce solids from about six months, night-time changes reduced, and we could leave her in Disana nappies and woollen pants through the night (go to Chapter 3 for more information).

Something you do need is some organised space to store toiletries and nappies so that you have everything at hand. A simple drawer system will work best. I keep the reusable wipes and all the parts of the nappy system, including coconut oil, in there.

---

207 https://www.nhs.uk/conditions/pregnancy-and-baby/washing-your-baby/

## *Yummy-time equipment*

A high chair enables your baby to take part in family meals from very early on, as soon as they can sit up for longer periods of time. This usually coincides with their ability to have food other than milk, and happens around the six months mark. For a high chair, plastic does come in quite handy, and at least it isn't single-use plastic.[208] There are lovely wooden ones, too. See if you can get them second-hand, but make sure all the parts are fully functional.

And this is about the only thing you will absolutely need. You won't need to clutter your cupboard with plastic plates, spoons and other types of cutlery – at least not in the early stages. One set of bamboo cutlery and a plate, bowl and cup are enough. I used some small bowls from my own crockery or old glass yoghurt jars when we first started.

# TIP 10
## Get a BPA-Free Soother – Or None At All

*Please, do something to switch that racket off!*

Love them or loathe them, I have used soothers only a few times until my daughter decided she didn't want them. And I was so grateful for it afterwards. She then found her fingers a lot more interesting, until she couldn't be bothered with sucking those any more either. At least she couldn't

---

208 https://www.ikea.com/gb/en/cat/highchairs-45782/

drop her fingers on the floor, and I didn't have to replace or sterilise them. I can remember getting somewhat frazzled trying to pick up dummies off the floor in Tesco's.

Your decision as to whether you want to use soothers or not depends very much on the baby, and sometimes it can be just the right thing for you or your partner to dip into a pool of calm even if it is only going to last for ten minutes. So, if you are thinking about using the soother or dummy (the latter derives from the less flattering term 'dummy teat'), it is wise to take care while you are establishing breastfeeding. The recommendation is to wait until you are both comfortable breastfeeding before you start using them, which would be about six weeks of age.[209] Otherwise, problems could develop with your milk supply because you may miss your baby's cues for their next feed. In one study, babies who used a dummy had an average of one less feed and spent around half an hour less feeding each day compared to those who did not. It is not clear, however, if dummies actually create the problem or if people who have issues already are more likely to use them. Babies who used a dummy also went around half an hour longer between feeds.[210] As part of ecological breastfeeding, frequent feeding is essential for lactational amenorrhoea to work as well.[211]

Soothers are also often claimed to reduce the risk of SIDS.[212] The intriguing fact emerged that the soother

209 https://www.laleche.org.uk/dummies-and-breastfeeding/

210 C. Aarts et al., 'Breastfeeding patterns in relation to thumb sucking and pacifier use' in *Pediatrics* 1999, Oct 1; 104 (4): e50.

211 Go back to Tip 1 for more information on breastfeeding and how it affects your fertility.

212 R. Y. Moon et al., 'SIDS and other sleep-related infant deaths: expansion of recommendations for a safe infant sleeping environment' in *Pediatrics* 2011, 128 (5): e1341–e1367.

stayed in the baby's mouth for about half an hour (probably the time it takes to fall asleep on the breast). This just means that the risk is higher when sleeping separately *without* a dummy, as opposed to sleeping separately *with* a dummy.[213] Ultimately, if you do need to use a soother, go for a product made from natural rubber.[214] Always check for splits and tears before you use them, though, and sterilise and replace them regularly.

# TIP 11

## Buy Ethical Clothing, or Clothes from Charity Shops, and Pass Things On

*Clothes Swap.*

It is one of the many dichotomies of our day and age that the more vocal the LGBTQ+ movement becomes, the more unicorns and whales and dinosaurs we see in children's clothes shops. It wouldn't matter so much if they weren't deliberately separated from each other, with one side standing out in pink and the other in blue[215].

Whenever I was so bold as to have my daughter dressed in a jumper with foxes on it, I would invariably be asked by strangers in cafes, or out shopping, "Oh, how cute. What age is he?"

---

213 R. Y. Moon et al., 'Pacifier use and SIDS: evidence for a consistently reduced risk' in *Maternal and Child Health Journal* 2012, 16 (3): 609–14 and P. Franco et al. 'Pacifier use modifies infant's cardiac autonomic controls during sleep' in *Early Human Development* 2004, 77 (1): 99–108.

214 https://www.sinplastico.com/en/128-dummies-and-teethers

215 https://www.letclothesbeclothes.co.uk/

And my stepmother would ever so often harp on: "She looks just like a boy in this jumper/suit/pair of trousers etc."

Another time, I had given in to my rebellious nature and fancied buying her a matching hat and scarf with whales (which were mostly in shades of grey and blue – as they are in nature) on them, and the shop assistant warned me, "Are you sure you want to buy this? It is from the boys' section…" When she saw how determined I was, all I got as a reaction was a big sigh. I mean, I was buying quite an expensive fashion item. Incredulous at her response, I handed her my debit card, which she accepted with a scowl disguised as a pitying smile.

But that is how off the mark I seem to have been with this. Why did I not buy the glitter/fairy/golden curls/unicorn cardigan? I don't know why.

But anyway, does my daughter 'look like a boy' in these things? She looks like neither sex, actually, no matter what she is wearing. It is all down to what we think clothes say about the wearer, not that the baby in those clothes has managed to shape-shift. Babies are gender neutral to start with (which isn't the same as being neuter). Do I look like a man because I'm wearing trousers? My grandmother probably would have thought so, and would never have worn anything else but skirts or trousers cut to a so-called 'feminine fit'. But we got past that stage, so why are we doing this to our babies?

## The practicalities of your baby's wardrobe
Theorising aside, a complete wardrobe for a baby consists of vests (the ones that have poppers along the crotch),

Babygros, cardigans, hats, scratch mitts and onesies to keep them warm. Later on, you can add more fancy stuff such as tights, dresses, jeans and jumpers. Babygros with fold-out gloves prevent your baby from scratching themselves, especially in the early days, and poppers are great. You can also look for those that fasten like a kimono, which are very handy if your baby doesn't like things pulled over their head. A Babygro and sleeping bag work very well for the night. Just pop a vest underneath when it is cooler. Padded jumpsuits or onesies are a must-have for the colder months. As soon as your baby starts walking, you can move on to footless onesies. And babies do not need shoes.[216] They should only wear socks or soft baby shoes to begin with, as long as they aren't able to walk. Better yet, let them wriggle their toes in the open air. According to some experts, shoes should be avoided entirely during childhood.[217] While this is not always possible, especially in colder weather, make sure that what you put on your baby's feet isn't too tight or constrictive. Happy Little Soles[218] make their baby shoes from chrome-free leather in Northamptonshire, the UK's traditional region for

---

216 If you want to buy shoes, go for some very soft chrome-free leather ones. Daisy Roots from Northamptonshire have a lovely range, allow for all-round foot growth so the toes can extend and wriggle about, and are checked with a metal detector for potentially harmful toxins. They are nice and soft and, what's more, also kind to wildlife and watercourses thanks to the omission of chrome in their production process. They all comply with British Standard EN 71-3.

217 https://www.ikea.com/gb/en/cat/highchairs-45782/

218 https://www.happylittlesoles.co.uk/products/brand-1/daisy-roots. html; also try for more leather-free options: https://www.toms. co.uk/;https://www.vivobarefoot.com/; https://www.greenshoes. co.uk/

shoemaking and they also do leather-free shoes which is the product of choice if you are vegan. Warm socks with anti-slip soles also work brilliantly in cold weather when indoors.[219]

It's a good idea to vary the sizes you buy as otherwise you will end up with lots of items all in one size, a lot of which your baby is never going to wear, and a lack of suitable clothes over the following months. If you buy or ask relatives and friends for larger-sized clothes, think ahead to the seasons or your baby will end up with clothes of the right size, but either too thick or too thin for the current weather conditions. For more expensive options, there is a chance to reserve these for special occasions and gifts.

### "Wind the bobbin up…" Who (and what) makes our clothes?

When I found myself back at Matalan (and I do occasionally, and they still get a better rating on Ethical Consumer than Tesco's F&F range, Primark, or Asda's George range),[220] I was thinking: *Who makes these clothes? And why are they so cheap? Is it ultimately really less expensive? What can I do to make this less damaging?*[221]

---

219 See Resources Directory for more on ethical clothing and footwear.
220 https://www.ethicalconsumer.org/fashion-clothing/shopping-
guide/clothes-shops
At the time of writing, the ratings were about to be reviewed. It is always worth checking for updates.
221 If you want to find out more, receive updates and take action for a fairer world of fashion, have a look at Fashion Revolution (https://www.fashionrevolution.org/about/get-involved/). Other ports of call are People Tree (https://www.peopletree.co.uk/) Natural Collection (https://www.naturalcollection.com/), and Greenfibres (https://www.greenfibres.com/).

And this brings us to the problem of pricing. When it comes to organic and ethical clothing, the problem is very often its affordability. Whenever I feel like buying so-called 'ethical clothing', I also feel like fainting at the prospect of being stripped of a month's wages only to end up with one Babygro and perhaps a pair of scratch mitts and a matching hat with baby bunnies on it. We are paying for the exclusivity of it and not just the heightened cost of manufacture when it is ethically done. Let us turn this round: is it ethical for these products to be so expensive? It should be normal, and consequently affordable, to be ethical.

## Materials

We are now so used to buying cotton clothes and those made from synthetic fibres such as polyester that it seems unusual to think of anything else. I am not advocating that we should now all buy what only very few of us can afford regularly, but I would like to raise awareness of what should be the norm for all our clothes.

Conventional cotton has usually been treated with bleach and is one of the most environmentally devastating crops we currently use. In the US, cotton has the third-greatest use of fertilisers and pesticides, surpassed only by soya and sweetcorn.[222] We need 150 g of fertiliser, and a regular spray of harmful pesticides including paraquat and parathion, to grow the cotton for one cotton shirt.[223] Now multiply this by the number of shirts you own

---

[222] https://gro-intelligence.com/insights/a-look-at-fertilizer-and-pesticide-use-in-the-us

[223] https://www.ncbi.nlm.nih.gov/pubmed/26196221 and http://www.who.int/heli/risks/toxics/bibliographyikishi.pdf

yourself. Try a rough estimate for all the shirts you have owned throughout your life. I stopped right there! About 29 million tonnes of cotton are produced each year, which equals twenty-nine shirts for everyone on earth. Not everybody owns twenty-nine shirts, however, so the lion's share goes to Western countries, who use an amount equalling one hundred shirts per person. Talking about inequality once more…[224] And consider this: while cotton grows on only 2.4 per cent of the land, it uses twenty-five per cent of all the fertilisers and ten per cent of all the herbicides in agriculture. Also, cancer rates are significantly higher in people living near cotton fields.[225]

We also seem to be quite obsessed with human-made fabrics, such as fleece, nylon and Lycra. It was genuinely revolutionary for our grandmothers and great-grandmothers when in the 1940s manufacturers first started using acetate cellulose to make rayon, acrylic and polyester fibres.[226] Their strong points are that they keep moisture away and are fast-drying,[227] which is why they are such popular materials for outdoor clothing, but they are not the right garments of choice for babies, as they can cause irritation on their sensitive skin and are not breathable materials.

---

224 https://www.theworldcounts.com/counters/cotton_
    environmental_impacts/world_cotton_production_statistics
    This website contains some more interesting facts. Just take a look
    at the steadily mounting figure of billions of tonnes of water used
    in cotton production.
225 https://ejfoundation.org/resources/downloads/the_deadly_
    chemicals_in_cotton.pdf
226 https://www.sciencehistory.org/distillations/synthetic-threads
227 https://www.whowhatwear.co.uk/worst-fabrics-for-skin

Organic cotton, bamboo, hemp and linen (although quite expensive) are the best alternatives to human-made, petroleum-based fibres and chemically treated cotton. Bamboo, for example, is a great thermal regulator, UV resistant and antibacterial, all of which make it great for nappies,[228] especially in the summer. Hemp, despite its bad reputation for its use in the narcotics industry, can yield 250 per cent more fibre than cotton.[229] It also suppresses weeds, which means fewer chemical pesticides are needed.

## Ethical, organic… and affordable

Instead of buying everything new, it is undoubtedly worthwhile to have a look round charity shops or on Facebook's marketplace, eBay or Oxfam's online shop, and often friends and family will help out and pass things on. The generosity of people can be astonishing. I've been gifted copious amounts of clothes, hand-me-downs kept in a community loop, usually as good as new, and you can always return the favour, if not to the person directly, then by doing the same for somebody else.

On the occasion that you are looking for special things, why not have a look at some organic, Fair Trade and 'un-gendered' clothing? Look out for the Organic Soil Association sign,[230] and the Global Organic Textile Standard.[231]

Frugi[232] have a lovely range of clothes, made using organic cotton fibres and only a small amount of human-

---

228 Look for these on http://www.naturebabies.co.uk/

229 https://www.votehemp.com/wp-content/uploads/2018/08/2_Industrial-Hemp_Superhero-Savior-of-Humanity.pdf

230 https://www.soilassociation.org/

231 https://www.global-standard.org/

232 https://www.welovefrugi.com/

made threads such as polyamide and elastane. They also donate one per cent of their turnover to charity. Their clothes feel soft and gentle on the skin, and they look sweet too. Moreover, they don't come colour-coded, which is very refreshing. John Lewis & Partners[233] also sell affordable organic cotton baby clothes. Look in the directory for more online retailers.

# TIP 12
## Get a Baby Carrier or a Simple Sling

*What do you mean, wear my baby?!*

Babywearing is a bit like breastfeeding and cloth nappies – once you get the hang of it, you wonder why everybody isn't doing it. It can seem a bit daunting at first as there is a mind-boggling number of systems to choose from to suit different requirements. It might leave you going around in circles before you make your decision, still wondering, *Is this the right one?* There is only one way to find out: try! The best thing is to visit a sling library[234] if you are unsure or wary of experimenting with babywearing yourself, until you and your baby have found out what suits both of you best. And be prepared to use different slings as your baby grows.

The following table includes the systems I have personally tried out, watching closely for my daughter's approval or if she was about to go on strike (her method of achieving this was very effective – she screamed the place down).

---

233 https://www.johnlewis.com/
234 Just a group where an old hand shows you the knack of a higher initiate. Look on Facebook or in the local directory.

| TYPES | BRANDS | COMMENTS |
|-------|--------|----------|
| Things with buckles. | BabyBjörn. Ergobaby. | Ease of use, but sometimes limited carrying positions. Very safe feel. Suitable for carrying older babies on the back (from about 5–6 months). |
| Woven wraps. | Baby Bird Handwoven. Storchenwiege. BaBy SaBye. | Lovely colours. Down-to-earth feel. Versatile. Problems can occur with slack when not tied correctly. A bit fiddly to start with. Steep learning curve. |
| Woven ring slings. | Maya Wrap. Baby Tula …and many more! | Limited carrying positions. Strain on the shoulder. Suitable for breastfeeding on the go. Fashionable. Useful for when the baby is still small and delicate. Light in the summer. |
| Stretchy wraps. | Kari Me. Caboo. Simple stretchy garment. | Slack can be a bit of a problem here, too. The Caboo is a hybrid of stretchy and ring slings, more readily adjustable than the other stretchy wraps. |

Table 6: *Types of Baby Carriers and Wraps*[235]

And what makes babywearing preferable to using a pram? A lot, as you will realise. The facts are on our side: carrying

---

235 For an exhaustive list go to https://www.wrapyouinlove.com/

infants for at least three to four hours a day is thought to reduce the duration of crying and fussy behaviour by as much as forty-three per cent by the time they are six weeks of age.[236] This is very possibly due to the closeness and gentle stimulation for the baby. They can hear your heartbeat, something they most probably experience as comforting as they associate it with their time in the womb. It also stimulates their digestive system. For you, it means hands free and the peace of mind of having your baby close to you. And it makes breastfeeding on the go a breeze. Most wraps come with instructions on how to leave a pouch for your baby to snuggle into and so enable you to feed discreetly. As another bonus, they are lightweight and easy to use most of the time. There will also be less of a need for so-called 'tummy time'. Playtime on their tummies became all important to protect babies' natural head shape when they started spending a lot of time sleeping on their backs as a result of the Back to Sleep campaign in the 1990s.[237] As long as your baby is sleeping on your chest, feeling the rhythm of your breathing and able to breathe freely themselves, there is no danger as with sleeping face down. But this is only the case as long as they are on your chest and nowhere else.[238]

There are a few basic rules to bear in mind to ensure your baby is carried safely. The authors of La Leche League's

babywearing-brands/

You might even feel inspired and make your own. Just Google 'make your own baby wrap'!

236 https://www.researchgate.net/publication/228383083_Natural_Parenting_-_Back_to_Basics_in_Infant_Care

237 https://safetosleep.nichd.nih.gov/

238 Look up the Safe Sleep Seven in La Leche League's *Sweet Sleep* (2014) (see Recommended Reading).

book *Sweet Sleep* came up with the acronym CHICKS. It stands for:

C    hin off chest
H    eld close
I    n sight
C    omfortable
K    issable head height
S    traight back[239]

In the early days, I found the Caboo the most practical wrap to use because of the rings on either side to fasten the two tails which go across your belly to form the pouch for your baby. A third, separate piece is tied around you and on top of your baby for extra safety. The advantage for beginners is that there is no 'complicated' wrapping involved. The disadvantage is that you can't do much else than carry on the front, as the hip carry is quite fiddly.

The main drawback with the Kari Me stretchy wrap is that you can't alter it much once you've tied it, although it might work for some. It largely depends on your shape and your baby's size.

Woven ring slings are a better option if you're not into stretchy. Your baby's weight holds them securely in the pouch. Make sure the cloth is tucked in nicely underneath baby's bottom, and their legs are in a so-called 'M shape'. Tighten the sling through the double ring, which should be positioned just in front of your shoulder and above your breast, so that some garment is pulled around your

---

239 This is an adaptation of TICKS from the UK Consortium of Sling Manufacturers and Retailers. Look up https://babywearing.co.uk, https://www.slingguide.co.uk and https://naturalmamas.co.uk

shoulder and goes across your back to keep your baby secure. The downside to this system is the strain on your shoulder as your baby gets heavier.

Woven wraps come in different sizes, and Size 6 is the most versatile as you will be able to use it for a long time and learn to tie it in many different ways. It is called Size 6 due to the length of the cloth, which is about six metres long. There are various ways of tying it depending on your baby's age and size, and your shape. YouTube tutorials come into their own for this.[240] Carry your newborn facing in and make sure their head is well supported.

If you are more into high-tech options, 'things with buckles' is the way to go. Clip-on baby carriers like BabyBjörn or Ergobaby[241] are excellent choices. When my daughter became heavier and I started carrying her on my back, I experimented a little with wraps before I became an Ergobaby devotee. My husband for one would never wrap, and prefers something he would call "a brilliant piece of kit".[242] And another tip: get teething pads (you can get organic cotton ones), which you'll have to order separately from their website, to wrap around the straps – they'll be chewed to bits otherwise.

Overall, keeping your baby close to you seems to be the best way to respond to their needs in the early stages until they gradually discover their independence, which they will do all too quickly.

---

240 For the long, woven wraps, watch tutorials like those found on
    https://www.wrapyouinlove.com or https://wrappingrachel.com
241 https://www.babybjorn.co.uk and https://ergobaby.co.uk
242 Look out for retailers such as https://littlepossums.co.uk, and for
    outdoor backpack carriers go to Tip 33.

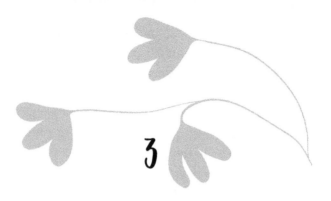

# 3

# Nappies

My cousin got a bit fidgety and sounded almost apologetic when I told her I was using cloth nappies. With a sidelong glance towards her fifteen-year-old son she said, "Well, I used Pampers. It never occurred to me to look for anything else." What she probably meant was: *I didn't even know there were other options*. In fact, these days we even call them 'Pampers' when we just mean nappies.

From my stepbrother, all I got was a plaintive moan: "Oh, what a hassle! I can't believe you are doing this!"

My father's initial response over the phone wasn't exactly encouraging either. "Oh, oh, oh!" he said, followed by a sharp intake of breath. "Have a rethink! Are you sure you want to do this?"

My reply was, "Yes. I have an electric washing machine. Granny didn't."

She wouldn't have had, in the 1940s, on a farm somewhere in Northern Germany. There had been a war on, and things didn't improve until sometime later. And that is how fickle human memory is. Another thing to note is this: people who suggest you shouldn't be using cloth nappies very often have no experience of using them on their children themselves (all be it that they may have been used on them when they were babies). With plumbing and electricity available it is really not as time-consuming as you might think. Just consider how many people in other parts of this world don't have access to these kind of amenities, and that will perhaps put it all back into perspective. And if the upfront financial outlay happens to stand in your way, the good news is you can apply for a grant with your local council to help you with this. These "real nappy schemes" are now run UK-wide and have been set up in the hope to reduce waste and encourage the use of cloth nappies as a more eco-friendly alternative.[243]

# TIP 13
## Use Cloth Nappies

*A brief lesson in nappy origami.*

If the thought of mountains of soiled nappies and damp indoor air in the winter from drying nappies on radiators makes you feel scared, read the ingredients list of disposable nappies first – and then return to the

---

243 http://www.fill-your-pants.com/councilnappyincentives.
html; https://www.thenappygurus.com/councilnappyschemes.
html; https://lizziesrealnappies.co.uk/blogs/council-incentives-
for-real-nappies; https://lizziesrealnappies.co.uk/blogs/
council-incentives-for-real-nappies

beginning of this chapter and consider the lesser of two evils. But don't worry: I won't be suggesting you use moss or milkweed to deal with your baby's excretions.

Cloth is a compromise between elimination timing and conventional disposables. The cloth napkin, or nappy as we know it, has been in use since the mid 19th century.[244] From then on, cotton became the preferred fibre for textiles. That is until the 1930s, when soft cellulose tissue made from wood pulp gave birth to the first disposable nappy. In the 1960s, real innovation with then-unknown implications hit the market like so many other things in those days. Polymer, a chemical compound of sodium polyacrylate which is so absorbent it can take up to eight hundred times its weight in water, was first used to make the disposable nappy we now seem to think is our only option. But there are convincing arguments against them – despite their alleged convenience.

**But why, then – tell me, please? Don't worry, I will. Or: why I wouldn't put my baby's health at risk for the sake of convenience**

1.  Cloth nappies are better for babies' skin and their overall health. This is mainly down to the different ingredients which are used to manufacture a disposable nappy. The following list includes all of them and their respective problematic implications.

---

244 https://www.darlingsdownunder.com.au/blog/nappy-versus-diaper and https://www.diaperjungle.com/pages/history-of-diapers

ADHESIVES: Glues are used to keep everything that constitutes a nappy together, including the little flaps that you use for fastening it. They may cause severe skin irritation.

SYNTHETIC FRAGRANCES: These are used to give the nappy a pleasant fragrance before the baby even fills it. They contain phthalates (plastic-based compounds) to prolong the life of the scent.[245] These may cause problems with internal organs such as the liver, kidneys and lungs, as well as the reproductive system.[246] The parabens contained in them can cross the skin and build up in the body over time. They are thought to mimic oestrogen and may trigger certain types of cancer. These concerns were discussed more openly after a UK study found residues in the breast tissue of breast cancer patients.[247]

PETROLATUM: This is a semi-solid mixture of hydrocarbons derived from petroleum.[248] It is commonly used for lubrication in medicinal ointments and is a jellylike substance also used as a barrier cream. It can be very drying to the skin.

POLYACRYLATE: This is by far the biggest culprit of them all.

245 https://toxtown.nlm.nih.gov/chemicals-and-contaminants/
      phthalates
246 https://www.theguardian.com/lifeandstyle/2015/feb/10/
      phthalates-plastics-chemicals-research-analysis
247 https://www.breastcanceruk.org.uk/science-and-research/
      background-briefings/parabens/
248 http://www.safecosmetics.org/get-the-facts/chemicals-of-concern/
      petrolatum/

Sodium polyacrylate is a by-product of the petrochemical industry and can take up to eight hundred times its weight in water.[249] This super-absorber keeps moisture away from your baby's bum, which of course is the most popular asset of disposables. But as it is very drying it can also act as a skin irritant. It won't break down in the soil, and if you come to think of it, that's not surprising as the fossil raw material used to produce it (yes, it's oil) has been lurking about for millions of years already. And another thing: it has been banned from use in women's sanitary products when a link between toxic shock syndrome and this ingredient became apparent[250] – if that doesn't set your alarm bells ringing, what will?

POLYESTER: These tiny plastic fibres inside the nappy are highly flammable and can cause respiratory problems and allergic reactions when released, in case of splits in the nappy.

POLYPROPYLENE: Another flexible plastic material which can cause respiratory problems if the nappy splits.

STEARYL ALCOHOL: A skin emollient which can be very drying to the skin.

WOOD CELLULOSE FIBRE: A product of the wood and paper industry and therefore natural. It is very absorbent. Manufacturers commonly use chlorine to bleach it,

---

249 https://www.chemistryworld.com/podcasts/sodium-polyacrylate/3007864.article

250 https://www.ncbi.nlm.nih.gov/pmc/articles/PMC3238331/ and https://healthwyze.org/reports/475-toxins-in-disposable-diapers-dioxin-and-sodium-polyacrylate

small quantities of which can remain in the nappy. The chlorine[251] may cause congenital disabilities, miscarriages and cancer, and is highly toxic in low doses.

Research by a German urological team published in the *Archives of Disease in Childhood* even suggests a link between disposable nappies and infertility in boys,[252] although this remains controversial.[253]

2.  Reusable nappies are far more benign for the environment. About 3–8 billion nappies[254] a day are filling up the landfill sites in the UK alone. They contain raw sewage, where bacteria and viruses thrive, and the plastic acts as a mini greenhouse in landfill sites. Also, viruses from recent vaccines, including the rotavirus (which causes a diarrhoea and vomiting bug) end up in the water tables.[255] In this case, the advantage of cloth nappies is that you can soak and disinfect them (which you wouldn't do with a disposable). In anaerobic conditions, disposables produce methane, which is thirty times more potent as a greenhouse gas than carbon dioxide.[256]

---

251 http://www.medicinesinpregnancy.org/bumps/monographs/
    EXPOSURE-TO-CHLORINE-IN-PREGNANCY/ and https://
    www.babygearlab.com/expert-advice/what-is-inside-those-
    disposable-diapers
252 http://news.bbc.co.uk/1/hi/health/941174.stm
253 https://www.theguardian.com/uk/2000/sep/26/sarahboseley
254 http://www.pollutionissues.co.uk/landfill-nappies.html
255 http://perintisjournal.weebly.com/uploads/2/6/5/7/26576870/
    paper_4__2017_vol._7_no._1_pp._43-58_.pdf
256 https://www.sciencedaily.com/releases/2014/03/140327111724.htm

3.  Reusable nappies place less of a strain on your budget after the initial investment, which can be a one-off payment of about £100–200, depending on which type you go for (see below). There are varying accounts as to how much a bag of say 30 Pampers, or Asda/Tesco/Aldi nappies etc. would cost.[257] According to Women's Environmental Network (WEN) research, the cheapest reusable combo would be terries, pants and pins for an estimated cost of about £50 upfront. That is opposed to a staggering estimated £940 for branded disposables such as Pampers that you would have to spend from the time they are born until your baby is old enough to use the potty or toilet as a toddler or pre-schooler.[258]

To get the numbers right: as opposed to the twenty-four cloth nappies you need, you're likely to go through six to eight thousand disposables before your baby is potty trained – or, as I would prefer to say, able to use the toilet, which means they are consciously able to control their bladder emptying and bowel movements. This means that we are thinking of forty black bin bags per year per child, and if you think, *Well, that's not too bad*, think of the total number of children in the UK and worldwide. It is difficult to give more than a rough estimate, but it is several billion!

257 https://www.netmums.com/coffeehouse/baby-794/babies-birth-12-
      months-58/1484274-how-much-do-you-spend-nappies-wipes.html
258 https://www.wen.org.uk/blog/2014/11/real-nappies-absorbing-
      lesson and https://www.theguardian.com/money/2015/jul/04/
      nappies-which-best-disposables-reusables-cost-ethics

4. There is evidence that cloth nappies are better for your baby's hips.[259] This was confirmed for me by the orthopaedic consultant who had a look at my daughter's hips when she was about five weeks old. According to her, it should be considered normal to use cloth nappies instead of disposables. Instead of midwives and pharmacists giving out more plastic packaging than items inside them to promote Pampers and Always sanitary products[260], they should talk more openly about a more sustainable approach.

5. Although there is less certainty about this, it is possible that toddlers using reusable nappies are more easily potty trained, but it could be that this is more down to your initiative than theirs as there isn't the 'convenience' of disposables.[261] It is also a good idea to invest in a reducer seat which helps them to copy your behaviour – which is to sit on a toilet – when they are old enough.

6. Most councils in the UK now offer incentives to reduce waste. If you contact them, fill in the form and send in your receipt, you can get at least some of the money you spend on reusable

259 https://www.thenappylady.co.uk/news/do-cloth-nappies-damage-your-babies-hips.html

260 Instead of Always, try sustainable sanitary products such as https://www.totm.com/, https://www.heygirls.co.uk/ and https://www.yoni.care/en/

261 https://www.mumsnet.com/Talk/potty_training/1183470-Potty-training-from-cloth-nappies

nappies back. Look at the Nappy Lady website for a comprehensive list to find out who to contact in your area.[262]

7. Contrary to common belief, disposables are more likely to cause nappy rash.[263] In the US, the rate for babies under twelve months increased from 7.1 to 61 per cent with the increased use of disposables.[264]

All I can say is that I haven't found that reusables present much of a hassle or a problem when we are out and about. I carry a bag to put the wet/dirty nappy in to take back home, and admittedly I do bring some disposables for an 'emergency' (see Tip 14). The main reason to use cloth nappies, though, is the feeling of being responsible for our children's future and their health and well-being. Looking at the evidence above, I think the facts are clearly on the side of old-fashioned cloth nappies. And with automatic washing machines at our disposal, I wonder why people feel it is going to lead to such an enormous workload. And even if you add up what extra you have to spend on washing powder/liquid and electricity, it is only one extra wash every other day on top of what I would typically do with the usual laundry of my own and my husband's clothes. I wash the nappies separately and use a big bucket

262 https://www.thenappylady.co.uk/council-subsidies.html and http://www.fill-your-pants.com/councilnappyincentives.html

263 https://www.theguardian.com/lifeandstyle/2014/may/09/why-i-prefer-to-use-cloth-nappies-and-cut-down-on-landfill

264 L. Fassa, *Green Babies, Sage Moms* 2008, p. 119; see Recommended Reading).

to soak them beforehand with Nappy Fresh sanitiser and stain remover from Bio-D.

# Yes, great, but which nappy is right for me?

I spent weeks researching this around the middle of my pregnancy. To help you avoid doing the same thing, look for a local nappy library or contact a nappy consultant (yes, they do exist) online. Just like with breastfeeding or babywearing, there are people out there to help you (mostly women, for obvious reasons – and I'm not being sexist). Most suppliers offer a questionnaire[265] to help you with the search for your ideal nappy.[266]

To give you a brief overview, here are the standard types you can choose from:

## *Terry nappy*

The most basic one of them all, and also the most versatile. The standard 60 x 60 cm size is the best value birth-to-potty option. If you have a very tiny baby, consider investing in some 50 x 50 cm or even 40 x 40 cm nappies.

It is essential to learn about different folds for different requirements.[267] The Nappy Lady[268] is a brilliant resource with several YouTube tutorials. You'll learn how to do a boy fold, which adds more padding at the front, or a girl fold, which has more padding at the back. The poo catcher helps

265 https://www.thenappylady.co.uk/advice-questionnaire.html
266 http://www.uknappynetwork.org/find-a-library.html
267 https://www.terrynappies.co.uk/folding-instructions/
268 https://www.thenappylady.co.uk

you deal with runny poo incidents, or try the butterfly fold, which is a flamboyant name for an elaborate fold which allows you to add extra padding if your baby is a heavy wetter. If this sounds a bit too much like nappy origami to you, stay with the simplest one. My personal favourite is indeed the origami fold, also known as the Chinese or easy fold (although I don't know about my daughter – if it were up to her there would be no nappy at all!).

Try and make sure they are made from one hundred per cent cotton, preferably organic, and try bamboo nappies in warmer weather.[269] Support local businesses and thereby reduce your carbon footprint even more.[270]

I used terry towels right from the start because they have some advantages compared to other reusable nappies. They are fast-drying, best if you're on a budget, can be used from birth until the toddler stage, and can even be upcycled as cleaning cloths afterwards. If you decide to go for this option, you will need the following items for a complete kit:[271]

1. The terry nappy – a square towel, roughly 50 x 50 cm in size, which you can fold according to requirement. The material of choice is usually cotton or bamboo.

---

269 https://www.naturebabies.co.uk

270 Try https://www.easypeasynappies.co.uk, https://www.naturebabies.co.uk or https://www.terrynappies.co.uk. Some of them are manufacturers and not just retailers. Brands like LittleLamb (https://littlelambnappies.com) also offer organic cotton or bamboo nappies, and manufacture in Turkey.

271 You can find complete starter kits on the Nappy Lady website to make your life and search easier. As you go along, you might want to try a few more things, but to start with, when you have lots of other things to think about, this is definitely helpful.

2. A washable liner (disposable paper liners have usually been added to the complete kit when you order them). You might have to order the washable liners separately at a little extra cost. A typical fabric used is fleece, as it is fast-drying. Better, although more expensive, options are hemp or an organic cotton mix.[272] I use hemp liners and bamboo boosters with my daughter's night-time tie-on nappies.

3. A Popo wrap.[273] There is a myriad of different brands to choose from. Reliable ones are Bambino Mio, Popolini, Bambinex or Motherease. They come in different sizes and go on top of your terry towel. You can choose between popper and Velcro fastenings, but simple pull-on pants are also available. I would recommend the XS size for newborns, and then you can move on to one-size nappies from about 5 kg (about 10 lbs) onwards as you can adjust the size with extra popper fastenings down the front of the pants. Apart from plastic/polyester ones, there are also wool pants available,[274] which I started to use at night when my daughter was about eight months old. I would compromise in this case,

272 Look on https://www.easypeasynappies.co.uk

273 Check the Resources Directory for more options.

274 https://www.plushpants.co.uk/popolini-wool-pant.html, https://www.cambridgebaby.co.uk/blog/?p=781, https://www.kingdomfluff.co.uk/wool-soaker-pants-c-205 and http://www.littlepants.co.uk/index.php?id_category=274&controller=category

however, as plastic comes into its own – and it's not single-use plastic, for a start.

4. Boosters for added absorbency. These are an absolute must for night-time nappies. Little Lamb[275] has some great boosters made from cotton or bamboo which you can fold into your terry. They really do the job.

5. Nappy Nippas for fastening the towel. These things look like a three-pointed seat belt and are used to hold the whole nappy bundle in place. Beware of the little hooks on each end. Do not let them dig into your or your baby's fingers!

6. Washable wipes. Get simple cotton pads. You can order them from the big reusable nappy retailers,[276] and they work best just with water – it is all you need.

One of the drawbacks of terry towelling is that it is quite bulky for newborns, especially if your baby is tiny. In that particular case, pre-folds are an excellent alternative (see below). And overall, terry can sometimes be a bit fiddly to use, especially when your baby grows and is sometimes quite uncooperative when it comes to being dressed. You will also find that the baby clothes we can buy off the shelves are, not surprisingly, designed to fit over a disposable these days. Vest extenders[277] can help to hold the whole bundle in place when buying pants a size larger.

---

275 https://littlelambnappies.com
276 See list in the Resources Directory.
277 https://www.thenappylady.co.uk/essential-accessories/vest-extenders.html

# Pre-folds

These are closest to terries in style. They are simple layered rectangles of cotton with a thicker layer in the centre, and need to be folded into thirds or pinned. Like terries, they require a wrap on top. They work very well with Bambino Mio wraps and are an excellent choice for newborns, especially when they are under 8 lbs, as terries are quite cumbersome (see above). You can fold them and slip them into the wrap.

# The all-in-one nappy and pocket nappies[278]

The easiest to fit and use, but they are also more expensive than the other types. Usually, they come with a Velcro fastening and everything else – padding, liner and cover – sewn together. They take longer to dry and have an exact fit, so you will go through several sizes before your baby is ready for the toilet. This means added cost and perhaps tumble-drying in wet weather because they take a lot longer to dry than the other types of nappies. They also have a shorter lifespan. And yet, they are very convenient at times. They may also be useful for the nursery or childminder. Another potential downside is their lack of reliability when it comes to runny accidents, as there is only one barrier, whereas with two-part or terry towels you have the liner, the nappy and the wrap on top, which is particularly essential for pre-weaned babies.

Pocket nappies, which go on just like an all-in-one, have an absorbent fabric part that is removable in the

---

278 Try Bamberoos (https://www.terrynappies.co.uk/bamberoos. html). Remember you will need a wrap on top.

wash – this means they are quicker to dry, and you may have more flexibility as regards the absorbency. They typically have a wrap, with a fleece liner permanently sewn in, leaving an opening at the back of the nappy, into which you can fit an absorbent liner. These come with a waterproof outer layer (cotton and fastenings), and a washable fabric insert which you can fold according to your baby's sex, and you can add extra padding at night.

## Two-part nappies or fitted nappies

These nappies are shaped more like a disposable nappy and may have fastenings such as Velcro or poppers. Sized nappies are available in more than one size (usually small and large). One-size or birth-to-potty nappies are fastened with poppers, Velcro, or a Nappy Nippa to adjust to your growing baby.

The sized fitted nappies are probably more comfortable to use than terries as there is no folding involved, especially with newborns, but they will end up being more expensive, as you need to buy two sizes. I tried the Diddy Diaper by Nature Babies. They are easy to line-dry in the summer and come either with Velcro fastenings or without, in which case you will need to use a Nappy Nippa. It is a great product and fits snugly underneath a wrap which can also be ordered from Nature Babies.

The birth-to-potty (one-size) option is cheaper but can look enormous on newborns, and tall babies might have outgrown them before they are ready for the toilet.

# Night-time

My personal favourite night-time nappy is the German-made Disana[279] tie-on nappy, which is an entirely different system from those I have already talked about. They might be less absorbent to start with, but they improve over time with several washes. The woollen over-pants need to be lanolised after each wash. The natural fibres neutralise the smell, which means that you won't have to wash them that often. I found that every one to two weeks was enough. As they are wool, you will need to wash them by hand. Don't let this put you off, though. At night, they work very well with an added Little Lamb bamboo booster and a washable liner to protect the tie-on nappy. Other options include a fitted bamboo nappy such as Bamberoos/Wonderoos[280] and a Motherease wrap if your child is a heavy wetter. You may also want to try the sized "Easy Peasy Bimble Nappy" by Easypeasynappies[281] which I can only recommend after using them on my daughter. It helped her feel a lot more comfortable during the night as a toddler.

## Hmm, and is that everything?

Apart from the nappies, you will also need a few more items to deal with them:

- A bucket in which to soak the nappies with eco-friendly sanitisers (use those without synthetic perfumes, chlorine bleach and optical

---

279 https://www.disana.de/en/collection/wickeln/
280 https://www.plushpants.co.uk/bamberoos-3-pack.html
281 https://www.easypeasynappies.co.uk/sized-nappies-2-c.asp

- brighteners). If they are not too badly stained, soak them with borax substitute, baking soda and vinegar to keep them soft and fresh.

- You may want to invest in a laundry net, which you can leave in the bucket to hold the nappies while you let them soak and then you can lift them out in one go and put them in the washing machine. Old-fashioned household tongs work very well too.

- I also decided to buy some reusable cotton wipes (just wet them in water), as some of the disposable wipes also present environmental and financial issues, as well as the matter of what you allow to come into contact with your baby's skin. I was quite happy to occasionally use Earth Friendly Baby Gentle Aloe Vera Wet Wipes,[282] which are one hundred per cent biodegradable. I stopped using wipes altogether when the runny-poo days had passed, and stuck to flannel and water, which went into the bag along with the soiled nappy. There are many alternatives to wet wipes such as flannels, reusable pads, muslins, wet tea towels or even just wet toilet paper– unscented and chemical free, and much more benign to your baby's skin and the environment.

## What about the extra wash cycles and my electricity bill?

Washing a nappy still uses five times less energy than making a disposable. What we often forget is that it's not

---

282 https://earthfriendlybaby.co.uk/

only about disposing of nappies, but also the resources which go into their manufacture. And there are other ways to minimise their impact on your electricity bill and the environment even more:

1.  Always wash on a full load (60 °C is usually enough for soiled nappies).

2.  Use eco-friendly detergents such as soap nut shells or home-made products.[283]

3.  Avoid using the tumble dryer and save that for emergencies. Line drying works best in the summer. The nappies smell fresh and clean, and UV rays bleach out stains and fight yeast build-up.

4.  Refrain from using fabric conditioner (you should anyway), thick nappy cream or bleach, and leaving dirty nappies lying around. Using washable nappy liners also extends the life cycle of your nappy.

## Elimination communication

If you are ambitious, you might even want to give elimination communication a go. Don't worry; it's not about eliminating communication – in fact, it's quite the reverse. The idea is to be very much tuned in to your baby's facial expressions and cues[284] to enable you to react promptly should they need to 'eliminate', or rid their body of digestive leftovers. You will have to react before they

---

283 See Chapter 6 for further details.
284 For more information, have a look at http://diaperfreebaby.
    org or https://www.naturalbirthandbabycare.com

have filled the nappy or just as they are about to do it. I found that some of it worked, at least occasionally, as long as you have a contraption of some description that looks a bit like a piece of loincloth[285] to catch any accidents – which are bound to happen. You will need to grab a good hold of your baby as they are hovering above the toilet bowl if you choose not to use a potty and they are too young to use a toilet with a reducer seat, which is likely to be the case before they are eighteen months old or so. I personally found that most of the ideas elimination communication is based on come into effect a little later and may not be suitable for the youngest of infants. From about eighteen months, my daughter began to occasionally point at her backside and say, *"Bau"* – which is the Malay word for 'smelly', which I had taught her because, according to my parents, that is what I used to say when I was growing up in Indonesia as a tot. Whatever you try, respond to your child's development and introduce the steps gradually. You can start by holding them above the toilet bowl to help them. I started doing this with my daughter when she was about six or seven months old. As soon as I could tell by the look on her face and the characteristic noises that an elimination was imminent, I held her above the toilet and loosened her nappy. Lots of praise and pointing out why I did this were included. Of course, that wouldn't happen every time, but increasingly it was the case. After having dealt with the runny poo in a newborn's nappy, I saw no reason why I should feel fussy about this.

---

285 https://littlebunnybear.com/

# TIP 14

## Try and Minimise Your Use of Disposables (and Use Eco Nappies on Such Occasions)

*My greenhouse legacy...*

Disposables do have their advantages; I have to admit that, despite everything that has been said previously in Tip 13. When you are travelling, looking for a childminder or asking friends or relatives to babysit, disposables are great and easy to use. When using Pampers, even only occasionally, still weighed too heavily on my conscience, I looked for a good and affordable brand of eco nappies. You can offset the slightly higher cost of eco-friendly disposables by using cloth most of the time.

When you choose a brand, make sure they meet the following standards:

- The wood pulp stems from renewable resources and is unbleached.
- They are one hundred per cent chlorine free.
- They either contain no gel which is sodium polyacrylate based, or at least include a biodegradable gel.
- They are latex free.
- They are breathable and kinder to the skin.
- They are fragrance free.[286]

---

286 For more information on fragrance go to Tip 16.

The Swedish Naty nappy is an excellent one I can personally vouch for, and you will notice the difference between their superb manufacture and conventional disposables. Other good brands are Beaming Baby, Rascal + Friends and Bambo Nature.[287]

It should theoretically be possible to compost eco nappies. If you do think about that, make sure you get the method of so-called vermicomposting right. This means that worms break down whatever you throw onto your compost heap to produce nutrient-rich compost. Microbes digest the worm casts and eliminate all the pathogens.[288]

I'm not so sure if dubious recycling schemes, such as the one launched in 2009, are on the right trajectory to assuage our guilt. A plant in Birmingham is supposed to be able to process thirty-six thousand tonnes of nappies a year.[289] The material can then be used for roof tiles, cycling helmets, shoe insoles and cladding. The methane that has been generated in the process is to be sold to the national gas grid by 2011. But it is probably much better not to waste all the resources that go into the production of millions of disposables, and even more energy to get rid of them again.

---

287 These all have high marks on Ethical Consumer for their overall product sustainability (environment, animals, people and politics). For more information also look on http://nappicycle.co.uk and https://ovoenergy.com (see directory for links).

288 M. Corkhill, *Green Parenting* 2006, p. 41; see Recommended Reading).

289 http://myzerowaste.com/2009/09/disposable-nappy-recycling-in-the-uk/ and https://www.letsrecycle.com/news/latest-news/uks-first-nappy-recycling-plant-opens/

# TIP 15
## Use Reusable Swim Nappies

*The seaweed is always greener.*

I have been using reusable swim nappies from the very beginning. I started taking my daughter to the pool when she was about six weeks old. I work part-time as a swimming teacher at the local pool, and I'm also a baby/ early years swimming teacher, and therefore I know about the mountains of nappies that end up in bins after just one session. The disposables the little ones are wearing as they come in and get changed before the session end up in those bins. Then double this figure with the disposable swim nappies. After a baby and toddler session, you have an average of about forty nappies with ten parent/baby pairs attending each class. And that is just at a 'wee' pool in south-west Scotland.

There is an excellent range of reusable swim nappies available, like Splash About and Konfidence.[290] These fit perfectly well underneath a baby wetsuit or costume/ trunks, and are leakproof. What you need is a cotton nappy wrap with a liner (the only bit that is disposable) and a cover, and on top of that, the swimsuit or wetsuit, although I would strongly recommend the wetsuit. Young babies in particular get quite cold when immersed in water for any length of time as they can't move their bodies very much by themselves. Some wetsuits are designed with four Velcro fasteners to make dressing and undressing your baby easier, and are called wraps where the arms and

---

290 https://www.splashabout.com/ and https://www.konfidence.co.uk/

legs remain free. They also ensure a better grip of your baby while you are in the water.

Some models of reusable swim nappy don't need a wrap or liners and just come as an integrated nappy and cover. These are usually one-size, but I wouldn't recommend those, at least not until when whatever ends up in there from the rear end is a little more solid. Especially with breastfed babies, you want them to be leakproof.

All in all, the kit will cost you £5 for the wrap and £8 for the cover. If you spend £1 for a swim nappy every time you go swimming (and usually the reusable ones will last you for several months even if you don't go for the one-size option), it isn't hard to work out how much money you will save. Check the size guide on the Splash About or Konfidence website carefully, though. My daughter had outgrown her first set by the time she was four months old.

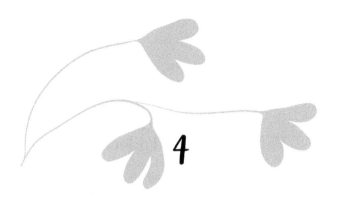

# 4

# Toiletries

When your baby is born, they will still be covered in the so-called vernix caseosa, which protected their delicate skin while they were immersed in water in the womb. This waterproof barrier is vital for protecting your baby against infections and skin irritations for the first few weeks after birth, which is why you shouldn't wash it off initially. Luckily, most hospital procedures have changed and now adhere to the so-called 'rooming-in' policy, which means that mother and baby won't be separated unless a medical emergency requires it.

The skin is our biggest organ and is genuinely marvellous in its capacity to regenerate, e.g. after a cut or scrape. It protects our vital organs inside our body. Exposure to skin irritants can potentially trigger lifelong problems, which is why we want to keep that to a minimum. Other than that, boycotting products which use palm oil, which is mostly unsustainably and unethically sourced, is another small contribution the consumer can make towards a more sustainable lifestyle.[291]

# TIP 16
## Buy Organic and Palm-Oil-Free Toiletries

*Or: what do saving the orangutan and my baby have in common?*

Let's be honest: you won't need a shelf stacked with enough products to equip a wellness and beauty studio to keep your little one's skin soft, supple and sweet-smelling. The ingredients lists of some of these products will make your head spin. Is such a chemical cocktail good, or even necessary at all, for our babies' delicate skin (or indeed anybody's)? You can purchase different bubble baths and body lotions, various brands of nappy cream and ointment etc. Which should you choose? Which are best for your baby?

Here is a rough guideline: the shorter the list of ingredients, the better. We want to look out for products that are fragrance free, organic, and free from parabens, phthalates, petroleum by-products, triclosan and sodium lauryl sulphate. So, what's the issue about all this?

---

291 https://littlegreenfootpath.com/2018/05/12/what-makes-cheap-vegetable-oil-unaffordable/

## The chemicals in everyday beauty products

FRAGRANCE: It seems nice to smell of roses, lemon, vanilla or lavender. But do you need a lot of artificial fragrance on your baby's skin? The problem arises when a lot of potentially harmful substances are lumped together under a general term, which in itself remains quite vague and elusive. Only twenty-six of the approximately two thousand fragrance chemicals in cosmetic products need to be named specifically in the ingredients list. So there are lots of issues when it comes to fragrances and their classification as "safe-to-use" ingredients.[292]

PARABENS: These come in various guises, such as methyl-, propyl-, butyl- and ethylparaben. They have been added to our creams and potions since about the 1930s to prolong their shelf life.[293] Nobody knows how harmful they are. Apart from causing rashes and allergies, studies[294] have shown that some parabens can mimic the activity of the hormone oestrogen in the body's cells. Oestrogenic activity is associated with certain forms of breast cancer, and parabens have been found in breast tumours. Hence, they are thought to increase the risk of breast cancer.[295]

---

292 https://app.croneri.co.uk/feature-articles/fragrance-classification-
    under-clp?product=135
293 https://www.good.net.nz/article/parabens
294 https://www.ncbi.nlm.nih.gov/pubmed/18484575
295 https://www.breastcanceruk.org.uk/science-and-research/
    background-briefings/parabens/, https://www.bcpp.org/resource/
    parabens/ and https://www.breastcancer.org/risk/factors/cosmetics
    A direct link between paraben exposure and tumours has
    been disputed on the NHS website: https://www.nhs.uk/
    news/2012/01january/pages/parabens-in-breast-cancer-tissue-
    studied.aspx

There is also some suggestive evidence that they interfere with male reproductive function and influence the development of malignant melanoma.[296]

PHTHALATES: Once you start reading the ingredients lists of some or most of the products you are using in your household, you are very likely to encounter phthalates: butyl benzyl phthalate (BBzP) and di-n-butyl phthalate (DnBP) to name but two.[297] They appear in everything from household cleaners and food packaging to fragrance, cosmetics and personal care products. But how hazardous are they? Some of them have been linked to Type 2 diabetes, obesity, breast cancer and ADHD, among other conditions.

PETROLEUM BY-PRODUCTS: One of the most popular additives from this category is propylene glycol,[298] which works as a moisturising agent in cosmetics. The problem with petrolatum or *paraffinum liquidum* is that toxins are not released from the skin when we sweat as the substances form a barrier by sealing our pores. On the other hand, the risk of absorption through your skin is minimal. You would need to apply it to broken skin (which means that the outer protective layer of your skin is missing) to risk it entering your bloodstream and thereby posing a threat to your health.[299]

---

296 http://www.ecocert.com/en and https://www.tandfonline.com/doi/full/10.1080/10408444.2017.1397099

297 https://toxtown.nlm.nih.gov/chemicals-and-contaminants/phthalates

298 https://www.orgaid.com/blogs/news/82910919-top-10-harmful-chemicals-to-avoid-in-skin-care

299 https://thebeautybrains.com/2014/10/whats-so-terrible-about-propylene-glycol/; https://www.beautifulwithbrains.com/is-propylene-glycol-dangerous/

TRICLOSAN: This works as an antibacterial agent. The implications of its use are horrendous; amongst them skin irritation, endocrine disruption, and bacterial and antibiotic resistance, as well as contamination of water and the resulting disastrous impact on fragile aquatic ecosystems.[300]

SODIUM LAURYL/LAURETH SULPHATE: This is the primary foaming agent in most of our cosmetic products. It is either synthetic or naturally derived from sources such as palm oil and coconut oil. The synthesising process happens by reacting lauryl alcohol with sulphur trioxide to produce hydrogen lauryl sulphate, which is then neutralised with sodium carbonate to produce SLS. This is a common ingredient of most of our household cleaning products, shampoos, conditioners, cleansing washes and even toothpastes. Depending on the concentration of the substance, it may cause adverse reactions if ingested or if it has been in contact with the eyes or skin. Conflicting reports on human and environmental toxicity from SLS have been published over the years.[301] The problem is not so much the small amounts contained in household cleaning products and personal care products, but prolonged and repeated exposure, which might indeed be harmful. Fears that SLS may have carcinogenic properties were mainly due to an allegedly misrepresented report of a chemical reaction between SLS and formaldehyde that

---

300 https://www.beyondpesticides.org/programs/antibacterials/triclosan

301 https://uk.lush.com/article/dont-stress-about-sls, https://slsfree.net/ and https://www.ncbi.nlm.nih.gov/pmc/articles/PMC4651417/

creates nitrosamines as a by-product.[302] Hence, it is best to stay with SLS derived from plant oils (preferably not palm kernel oil) and to keep exposure to a minimum.[303]

As we can see, it is probably best to go back to basics – and cheaper, too. Consumers can also take matters into their own hands by avoiding products packaged in Recycling Code 3 plastic and those that include the vague ingredient 'fragrance' on their label, and by purchasing organic products packed in glass as much as possible.[304]

## *Products for your baby's beauty regimen*

To make sure your baby is well looked after, limit yourself to the following products:

NAPPY CREAM: There are various organic brands.[305] Burt's Bees, Weleda, Beaming Baby and Organic Babies are all excellent choices. Organic Babies, the most expensive of these, is one hundred per cent organic and made without parabens, lanolin, phthalates, artificial perfumes, petrochemicals and colourants. Burt's Bees only state that

---

302 https://www.ncbi.nlm.nih.gov/pmc/articles/PMC4651417/
303 As the authors of a 2015 article in *Environmental Health Insights* (see previous footnote) state: 'From a sustainability and environmental health perspective, sourcing surfactants such as plant-derived SLS avoids incurring the additional environmental and human health impacts caused by the extraction of petroleum and the production of petrochemicals.'
304 https://www.theguardian.com/lifeandstyle/2015/feb/10/ phthalates-plastics-chemicals-research-analysis
305 https://www.biggreensmile.com/departments/nappy-creams. aspx?deptid=NAPPYCREAMS

their ingredients are one hundred per cent natural, but, being slightly less expensive, their cream is still very much worth trying. Weleda list ninety-two per cent organic ingredients in their ointment. And the best cure for nappy rash is entirely free: fresh air!

BABY LOTION OR OIL: I have only used Kokoso on my daughter's skin so far. Coconut oil, which is about ninety per cent saturated fat, tends to solidify in cold weather, so you will need to let it melt in your hand before applying. During the hot summer months, however, it will sometimes almost turn into a liquid. You can pop it in the fridge to let it become solid again, if you like. I for one was quite happy when it was softer in warmer weather, as I felt it was easier to apply. I found it works very well with baby massage.

MILD LIQUID SOAP: I was delighted to use Kokoso fragrance-free hair and body wash on my daughter's skin by the time she was six weeks old. Before that, I had used plain water and a konjac sponge (see Tip 17). The list of ingredients for the Kokoso wash is about half the length of those of other baby skincare products, and the managing director assured me in an email that the vegetable glycerine used stems from sustainably sourced palm oil. Kokoso have recently added a solid bar of gentle baby soap to their range, which will reduce your plastic footprint even more. Make sure you check your local recycling options.[306]

---

306 https://www.greenmatters.com/renewables/2018/09/13/ZG59GA/
    plastic-recycling-numbers-resin-codes

MINERAL SUNSCREEN:[307] With so many different products out there, it is difficult to know which one to choose.[308] Some are quite pricey, but worth the extra cost for various reasons. Organii Baby by the Natural Skincare Company[309] is a highly effective lotion which has been specifically designed with babies and very young children in mind. As a UVA/UVB filter, it uses Pongamia extract or pongamol.[310] Titanium dioxide and zinc oxide have been added as mineral filters.[311] This product is good if you are looking for a higher SPF; it has an SPF factor of 50+. One of the downsides is that some of the ingredients are not specified as organic. One example is stearic acid. Is it derived from coconut oil? Or is it from palm oil? If so, has it been sustainably sourced? Another one is that to increase the product's fluidity, the emulsifier polyglyceryl-3 polyricinoleate[312] also appears in the ingredients. These are all things you will most probably be seeking to avoid! Organic Children sunscreen by Green People[313] is eighty-four per cent organic and is sold in fully recyclable and carbon-neutral plant-based packaging. As a bonus, 30p is donated to the Marine

---

307 Read more at https://littlegreenfootpath.com/2019/06/29/top-natural-sunscreen-brands-and-homemade-diy-sunscreen/
308 https://www.biggreensmile.com/article/our-safest-natural-sun-cream-for-babies-and-children.aspx
309 https://www.thenaturalskincarecompany.co.uk/organii-sun-milk-spf50-for-babies-and-sensitive-skin-125ml/#product-description
310 https://www.ewg.org/skindeep/ingredient/722640/PONGAMOL/
311 https://kabanaskincare.com/faqs/what-is-the-difference-between-titanium-dioxide-and-zinc-oxide/
312 https://en.wikipedia.org/wiki/Polyglycerol_polyricinoleate
313 https://www.greenpeople.co.uk/

Conservation Society[314] with every tube purchased. It's one of the few sunscreens that don't inflict any damage on reefs and other marine life. It is also gentle enough for those with skin conditions such as psoriasis or eczema. It contains aloe vera, edelweiss and beeswax, and is therefore non-greasy, water repellent and scent free. Unfortunately this sunscreen is not entirely suitable for very young babies, and if you are vegan you may object to the beeswax contained in it. It also has a slightly lower SPF (SPF 30). The emulsifiers are at least all plant-based: cetearyl alcohol (an emulsifying plant wax), glyceryl stearate (a plant-derived emulsifier) and cetearyl glucoside (another plant-derived emulsifier). With babies younger than six months, it is best to refrain from using sunscreen altogether if possible, as only very few products are suitable for their delicate skin. It is always best to cover them in light clothing and to stay in the shade or indoors during the midday hours instead of slathering on the sunscreen. And as another possible DIY project, why not try and make your own? Pronounce's recipe makes a safe and very reliable sunscreen without the nasties![315]

All of these products can be used in small quantities. An infant under six weeks will only need warm water (up to 37 °C) to keep them nice and clean. And it is still going to be fun, even without loads of bubbles. You might also enjoy some more natural bath time ideas, especially when you are looking for a soothing, mineral-oil-free

---

314 https://www.mcsuk.org
315 https://pronounceskincare.com/diy-sunscreen-easy-make-need-recipe/

option in case of nappy rash or other skin problems. Oat and wheatgerm baths are gentle, SLS- and toxin-free options with the added benefit of natural healing properties. If you are worried about the bits getting stuck in your baby's hair, you can still gently rinse them off after the bath – and remember to put a sieve on top of the drain! As an alternative, put the ingredients in a clean sock and squeeze all the goodness out into the warm water.

## For an oat bath:

Add 3–4 tbsp of rolled oats (preferably organic) to your baby's bathwater. This helps with minor skin problems such as redness and slight inflammation.

## For a wheatgerm bath:

Add 50 g (2–3 oz) of wheatgerm to your baby's bathwater. Wheatgerm contains Vitamin E, magnesium and zinc, and therefore supports gentle and natural healing of minor skin problems like nappy rash and baby acne. For more protein content, add about 10 ml of your own milk, or fresh whole cow's or goat's milk if you prefer.

These tips should, of course, never be used on their own if your baby suffers from more severe skin conditions. But as a soothing alternative to a bath with lots of chemicals which would potentially only aggravate the problem, I found it did the trick. These natural bath ideas work very well for you, too.

# Ask the expert:
# Lauren Taylor, Kokoso Baby skincare

It is a good thing that we have become more and more aware of the negative effects of the chemicals contained in our everyday personal care products, both on our health and the environment. This is even more crucial when it comes to young babies. At the forefront of this movement are people like Lauren and Mark Taylor, who started their business from scratch with almost no marketing budget and then went on to pitch it to the 'Dragons' in May 2016. Their efforts were crowned with successfully getting Touker Suleyman on board. They also received very positive reactions from Deborah Meaden and Sarah Willingham.[316]

This marvellous brand is appealing in its simplicity and minimalist approach. But let's see what Lauren can tell us herself about her fabulous products in her own words.

*What inspired you to start your business?*

As a new mum, I was worried about hidden nasties in mainstream baby toiletries. My little girl had very sensitive, eczema-prone skin and I wanted to find a skincare solution I could trust completely. I researched coconut oil and discovered that it's the only natural oil that independent dermatology nurse Julie Van Onselen recommends for baby skin.

I had never used coconut oil before, but I was amazed at how wonderful it was for my baby's skin whilst being so versatile, natural and pure. I quickly became passionate

---

316 Read more about their success story at https://kokoso.co.uk/blog-1/kokoso-baby-softens-up-the-dragons

about sharing its many benefits and uses with others, and started buying jars for friends with babies. That's when I had my light-bulb moment: I would create my own premium-quality organic coconut oil brand that new parents like myself could trust to be the very best product for their babies' skin. And so Kokoso was born.

*What sets your products apart from conventional baby skincare products?*

Each of our award-winning products harnesses the amazing skincare properties of our very own premium organic coconut oil. We blend this with only the highest quality, most naturally effective ingredients such as organic aloe vera and organic shea butter, as well as gentle natural active ingredients like celery seed extract (for cradle cap) and plant sugars (for skin hydration).

When it comes to our ingredients, we firmly believe in quality over quantity. In addition, we ensure every single ingredient in our range achieves a green rating for safety on the Skin Deep® Database[317]. As parents of babies with sensitive skin, we know how important it is to have transparency and peace of mind when it comes to the formulation of baby skincare products.

*What are the main properties of coconut oil and how are these beneficial for babies and very young children?*

As one product with so many uses, there really is nothing better than coconut oil to care for babies' skin. Not only

---

317 The database is part of the Environmental Working Group (EWG) and is an excellent way to check if the products in your bathroom cupboard are safe to use and eco-friendly: https://www.ewg.org/skindeep

is it an excellent natural emollient and massage oil, it also boasts anti-inflammatory, antibacterial and antimicrobial properties. Lauric acid, one of the key components of coconut oil (and breast milk), is known for its amazing natural healing powers. It's why it's so incredibly good at soothing the many minor skin complaints little ones experience in their first year of life, from baby acne and nappy rash to dry skin and eczema.

*Please, tell us more about your company's pledge to sustainability.*

We're extremely passionate about making the best products for both baby and planet, so we run our business with strong ethics and eco-friendly values. We formulate with high-quality organically farmed ingredients that are safe and gentle for babies, children and the environment.

Our coconut oil is sustainably and ethically produced from zero-waste premium organic coconuts, we use recyclable packaging for all of our products and we're continuously investigating the latest innovations in environmentally friendly packaging.

We have two new products launching in 2020; one packaged in an innovative cardboard tube and the other in post-consumer recycled plastic – aka recycled milk bottles! In addition, the packaging for our gift sets is made from responsibly sourced wood and has a biodegradable film window derived from wood pulp, so you can pop it in the food waste at home.

When we send out parcels we use biodegradable packing peanuts and environmentally friendly cushioning paper. Where we can, we always use recycled packing tape.

Our natural konjac baby bath sponge is one hundred per cent biodegradable and sustainable. And we even drive an electric company car that we charge up through solar panels!

# TIP 17
## Use Sponges, Hairbrushes and Toothbrushes made from Natural Materials

*It all grows on trees – literally!*

Have you ever heard of the konjac sponge?[318] I hadn't. But once I started using it to wash my baby, I became a convert. It works beautifully from the very first bath you give your baby, and is completely natural. The konjac potato, or *konnyaku*, is a perennial plant native to Asia and can be found growing wild at high altitudes. It hardens when it dries, so you need to leave it in water before use so it can become supple and soft. Kokoso sell these sponges as part of their baby skincare range.

Another thing you will need is a soft baby hairbrush. Look for a wooden one with natural fibres. The Kokoso baby hairbrush is made from beech wood and can be used to comb your baby's delicate hair and also gently exfoliate the skin. It works well in conjunction with coconut oil to help with cradle cap (see Tip 20).

As soon as your baby's first tooth appears, it is wise to think about proper dental hygiene. Conventional plastic

---

318 https://www.konjacspongecompany.com/

toothbrushes should be avoided for various reasons, not only because of the plastic waste they create. They are also quite challenging to handle with young babies. The Jack n' Jill silicone finger brush is an excellent product.[319] You can slip it onto your finger like a thimble and use the brush side to clean your baby's first teeth and the dimple side to massage sore gums – which they are bound to have when they are teething. These brushes come in a case and are therefore convenient when travelling. You can also chill them in the fridge to relieve teething discomfort, and they are easy to sterilise in sterilising solution. The best thing about them is that they are BPA-, PVC- and phthalate free, being made of one hundred per cent food-grade silicone. Order them online, and you receive them in biodegradable packaging made from recycled paper board with a cornstarch window. These silicone toothbrushes come in three stages. Stage 3 is for toddlers, so we are only going to have a look at Stage 1&2 in this context. You can move on from the finger toothbrush (Stage 1) as your baby grows. I found my daughter was biting down on my finger with her six little teeth by the time she approached her first birthday. I then decided it was time to move on to Stage 2. This looks like a proper toothbrush but has a slip-on ring to prevent the brush being pushed too deep into the mouth when the baby wants to try using it by themselves.

The current recommendation for children under three years is to have their teeth brushed twice daily, with a smear of toothpaste containing at least 1,000 ppm fluoride.[320] There are two schools of thought concerning

---

319 https://www.jackandjillkids.com/

320 https://www.nhs.uk/conditions/pregnancy-and-baby/looking-after-your-infants-teeth/ and https://www.nhs.uk/conditions/fluoride/

fluoride. Fluoride seems to be essential in preventing tooth decay.[321] Contrary to this, there have also been some concerns that fluoride may be responsible for a variety of health conditions.[322] A condition called dental fluorosis can sometimes occur if a child's teeth are exposed to too much fluoride when they're developing. Mild dental fluorosis can appear as very fine pearly white lines or flecking on the surface of the teeth. Severe fluorosis can cause the enamel to become pitted or discoloured.[323]

Ultimately, the very best way to look after your baby's teeth and prevent tooth decay is to reduce their intake of sugary foods. Don't give your baby sweet drinks, not even fruit juices; offer water or unsweetened milk instead.

# TIP 18
## Go Easy on Using Toiletries Yourself

*And instead of Cleopatra's mare's milk,
try other natural products!*

When you want to freshen yourself up a bit (and of course, we all do sometimes), try and either find organic brands or make some products yourself at very little time and cost. It is easier than you think and can be part of embarking on a new lifestyle (which won't mean you have to wear Birkenstock sandals from now on if the thought makes you want to run or hide – or both!). The products to look

---

321 https://www.nhs.uk/conditions/fluoride/
322 https://www.medicalnewstoday.com/articles/154164.php
323 https://www.nhs.uk/conditions/fluoride/ and https://www.healthline.com/health-news/you-shouldnt-buy-fluoride-free-toothpaste#1

out for are free from parabens, phthalates, petroleum by-products (this includes Vaseline), sodium lauryl sulphate, triclosan and fragrances, so this is pretty much what you would be doing for your baby. Just go back to Tip 16, and you'll see why.

## *The smell of roses*

No one suggests you shouldn't smell fresh and lovely yourself, but your baby prefers *your* smell. They react to it, and, in this case, nature truly is best. Consider buying some fragrance-free skincare and haircare products. Instead of heavily, artificially fragranced body lotion, some natural oils, such as Vitamin E, avocado, olive, safflower and others, are a better choice depending on your skin type.[324] Alternatively, MooGoo Skincare[325] sell a broad range of natural products which are designed especially for people with skin problems.

Look for alternatives such as a crystal deodorant made from rock salt or ammonium alum sulphate. Sweat is the natural way for the body to excrete toxins. These crystal sticks neutralise bacteria that cause your sweat to smell, rather than clog your pores like a lot of conventional deodorants will. Or try natural deodorants by Earth Conscious,[326] who are based on the Isle of Wight, or even go DIY.[327] And it might be an idea to ditch the

---

324 https://www.schoolofnaturalskincare.com/essential-oils-for-skin/ and https://www.everydayhealth.com/skin-and-beauty/best-natural-oils-healthy-skin/

325 https://moogooskincare.co.uk/

326 https://www.earthconscious.co.uk/
    10p from the sale of every deodorant goes to marine conservation (find out more on their website).

327 Find out more on my website https://littlegreenfootpath.com/

commercially bought perfume as they very often contain phthalates to make the smell last longer on your skin.[328] There are a lot of specially formulated perfumes available that contain fewer harmful chemicals.[329]

## *Golden tresses*

Thanks to the rush of hormones during pregnancy, your hair may still look very nice and thick and shiny for a while after you have given birth. As for shampoo, look out for organic ingredients or use a shampoo bar. The Friendly Soap[330] range smells lovely and does the trick. Another impressive product range is Stop the Water While Using Me![331] They even sell conditioner bars.

It might take a while to get used to these products, and your hair might produce a little more oil (or sebum) to begin with, which is its natural way of taking care of itself. It is better to try different products to see which one works best with your hair, just as you would do with conventional shampoos. You might even want to think about ditching shampoo altogether or perhaps only using it occasionally, e.g. after a swim in a pool to get rid of the chlorine in your hair.[332] Any adjustments will settle down after a while and you'll probably feel the better for it. And instead of liquid body wash, use the good old bar of soap again, but look for palm-oil-free options, or ones made

---

328 https://www.forceofnatureclean.com/truth-about-toxic-fragrances/
329 https://www.edenperfumes.co.uk/about
330 https://www.friendlysoap.co.uk/
331 https://stop-the-water-while-using-me.com/de/
332 https://littlegreenfootpath.com/2019/01/26/steps-to-a-shampoo-free-hair-care/

with sustainably sourced palm oil.[333] Brands like Suma still contain glycerine made from palm oil, which appears as vegetable oil in the ingredients list.[334]

Also, be mindful of your exposure to certain types of hair dye. A lot of different brands of hair dye contain paraphenylenediamine (PPD), a carcinogen, and peroxide and ammonia, which can both be harmful to the developing baby during pregnancy and very possibly afterwards as well. Research by Greenpeace[335] on blood taken from umbilical cords was able to establish high contents of a variety of chemicals such as triclosan, brominated flame-retardant TBBPA, phthalates, artificial musks, BPA, alkylphenols and organochlorine pesticides (e.g. DDT), which shows how harmful chemicals can cross the placental barrier. It is difficult but not impossible to find permanent dyes without PPD. Ammonia is not present in a number of dyes, and nor is peroxide. If you still feel that dying your hair is something you cannot do without, you may want to check out some of the safer options.[336]

Another possibility is to try natural hair dyes, such as henna, which can give your hair beautiful earthy-looking colours[337], or highlight your hair with camomile.[338] If you

---

333 https://www.ethicalconsumer.org/palm-oil/palm-oil-free-list

334 https://littlegreenfootpath.com/2018/05/12/what-makes-cheap-vegetable-oil-unaffordable/

335 https://www.ncbi.nlm.nih.gov/pubmed/13542098, https://www.ncbi.nlm.nih.gov/pubmed/21349779 and https://www.ewg.org/research/body-burden-pollution-newborns

336 https://directionshaircolour.co.uk/

337 For henna try: https://uk.lush.com/products/henna-hair-dyes.

338 Some people have had good results with sage to cover the first grey hairs appearing: https://www.hairbuddha.net/sage-tea-to-darken-grey-hair/.

use henna, stay with the natural one and refrain from using certain black henna products. These very often contain PPD just like other hair dyes, with Henna noir by Lush being a notable exception.[339] Although its use is permitted in hair dyes in the EU, it is strictly controlled.[340]

The issues with nail polish and nail polish remover are that they contain several toxic chemicals, amongst them toluene, formaldehyde and ethyl methacrylate (EMA) which can either cause cancer or be harmful to your unborn child. Some traces have also been found in samples of breastmilk.[341] The main concern is for workers in beauty studios who will be exposed to fumes and will be handling products throughout their working day. But even if your exposure is minimal, it is probably wise to be cautious. If you don't want to do away with it altogether, you may want to try alternatives with fewer harsh chemicals.[342]

## *Dental care*

Toothpaste can be problematic as it almost always contains sodium lauryl sulphate.[343] Weleda has a very good range of natural toothpastes, which are free from fluoride, preservatives, artificial colourants and flavours. You may

---

339 https://uk.lush.com/products/henna-hair-dyes/noir-henna

340 https://www.nhs.uk/live-well/healthy-body/black-henna-neutral-henna-ppd-dangers/

341 https://www.huffingtonpost.co.uk/entry/nail-polish-chemicals-entering-the-body_n_5627e311e4b02f6a900f59c7; https://www.ncbi.nlm.nih.gov/pubmed/24630247; https://www.ncbi.nlm.nih.gov/pubmed/24316320

342 https://fairypants.co.uk/product-category/cosmetics/nail-varnish/

343 https://www.ncbi.nlm.nih.gov/pmc/articles/PMC4651417/

also want to try alternatives such as tooth powder,[344] which is SLS-, glycerine- and fluoride free. Another brand to look out for is Georganics,[345] who make a kaolin-based and fluoride-free toothpaste. You apply it to your toothbrush with a little bamboo spatula as it comes in a glass jar instead of a plastic tube. It might be an idea to mix and match again, to reduce your exposure to potentially harmful chemicals but still ensure the remineralisation of your teeth. Oil pulling[346] with oils such as coconut oil as part of your oral hygiene routine is another natural way of taking care of your teeth and can be used in conjunction with the organic toothpaste and the natural toothbrushes listed below.

An alternative to the all-plastic toothbrush is the bamboo toothbrush. The bristles are still made from nylon fibres, as there is currently very little else that does the job equally well. There is a natural alternative available with boar bristles.[347] The downside to these is that they can get quite smelly after a while. Neither are they suitable for vegetarians or vegans. You can order bamboo toothbrushes in bulk and snap off the head when your brush is past its use-by date. Save Some Green,[348] The Humble Co.,[349] Hydrophil[350] and Truthbrush[351] are all great products to suit anybody's needs and tastes, which make you wonder

---

344 https://www.goingzerowaste.com/blog/dentist-approved-toothpowder-recipe-brush-with-bamboo
345 https://georganics.com/collections/toothpaste
346 https://www.ncbi.nlm.nih.gov/pmc/articles/PMC5198813/
347 https://ecotoothbrush.wordpress.com/tag/boar-bristle/
348 https://www.savesomegreen.co.uk/
349 https://thehumble.co/
350 https://hydrophil.com/en/
351 https://www.thetruthbrush.com/

why we have been using plastic toothbrushes for so long.[352] If you use an electric toothbrush, there are at the time of writing no bamboo products available. As an alternative to Oral-B, you may want to try LiveCoco[353] or Brushette[354] – we've got to start somewhere!

352 Find out more about these products in my blog post: https://littlegreenfootpath.com/2019/09/23/eco-friendly-bathroom-step-2-dental-care/
353 https://www.livecoco.com/
354 https://eu.brushette.com/

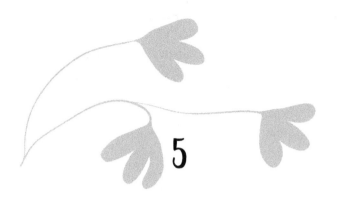

# 5

# Health and Medication

Did you ever think about the fact that the pharmaceutical industry is a lot of the time only reproducing what Mother Nature already offers us? I by no means want to decry medical advances and their benefits that we have seen in recent history, but for everyday little aches and pains, we can support the self-healing properties of our body more gently.

You may want to look into some holistic therapies and remedies for minor ailments, or as part of a lifestyle which is thought to prevent common illnesses before they even occur. There is not always a direct correlation, but a lot of our ailments are due to an inactive, sedentary lifestyle and eating the wrong foods. Minor issues very often don't require any significant intervention, and it is crucial to allow the body sufficient time and rest to heal itself. That said, a balance should always be maintained, and always seek medical assistance when it is required.[355]

---

355 If you are worried about the safety of certain medications, have a look on https://toxnet.nlm.nih.gov, https://kellymom.com and https://www.breastfeedingnetwork.org.uk

Medical herbalists, acupuncturists and reflexologists can very often help a great deal with rebalancing the body. Their approach differs in many ways from the norm in our society, but that doesn't make them less effective if applied correctly for the right things at the right time. It is important to note that all therapies have their place, but overuse of antibiotics can have serious effects such as antibiotic resistance, which is currently on the rise.[356]

# TIP 19
## Try Alternative Remedies

*Nature's treasure chest 1.0.*

## *Arnica*

Arnica is very good for treating bruises and reducing swelling. It is available as a homeopathic ointment or tablets. Find it on Weleda's website,[357] although there are a variety of different brands available to suit your preference.

## *Bach Rescue Remedy (Five Flower Essence)*

Several drops on the tongue or in a glass of water can relieve shock and distress. It works well during labour, too. Find it on Healing Herbs.[358]

---

356 https://www.who.int/news-room/fact-sheets/detail/antibiotic-resistance
357 https://www.weleda.co.uk/natural-ingredients/lead-plants/arnica
358 https://www.healingherbs.co.uk/using-bach-essences/question-answers/what-is-five-flower-essence-copy/

## Honey

A powerful antiseptic which has been in use for millennia. You can apply it to minor burns or use it in combination with lemon to relieve symptoms of colds such as a sore throat. It also works on small cuts and enhances the healing process. Be aware, however, that babies under twelve months should never ingest it as it is raw, i.e. not pasteurised, and may contain spores of the bacterium *Clostridium botulinum.*[359]

## Lavender oil

Calming and soothing; use a few drops in your bathwater or on a hanky at bedtime to help you sleep.

## Tea tree oil

Famous for its antiseptic properties, tea tree treats blemishes on your skin (so is great for teenagers). You can also use it on cuts and sores, and a few drops diluted in water work as an antibacterial rinse.

## Calendula cream

Use this to soothe minor cuts and grazes. Try Nelsons calendula cream,[360] which is widely available online or at various stockists.

---

359 https://www.nhs.uk/conditions/botulism/
360 https://www.nelsons.net/en/our-brands/nelsons/nelsons-skincare/
    calendula-cream

## *Oats*

A handful of oats in a muslin bag or a sock under the hot water tap as you are running your bath can soothe many skin conditions such as eczema (see Tip 16 for baby's bath).

## *Citronella*

Mix Citronella into witch hazel and glycerine. It works as a mild insect repellent. Only use it on babies' or toddlers' clothes. This is my preferred recipe:

- About 50 ml water
- 50 ml witch hazel
- 1 tbsp vegetable glycerine
- About 20–30 drops vanilla extract, citronella and eucalyptus oil per 100 ml of liquid

## *Frozen peas*

Use a pack wrapped in a towel as a cold compress.

## *Millet or rice*

Use uncooked in a sock as a heat compress for a sore back or shoulder. Stick it in the microwave for two minutes on medium heat.

## *Mild disinfectant gel*

Try not to overuse disinfectant gels and hand sanitisers. Use them sparingly and wisely. Opt for a probiotic mixture, including lovely-smelling and sanitising essential oils instead. Please do not use this recipe on your baby's delicate skin. It is primarily meant to be for your own use, for example after a nappy change if there are no handwashing facilities available. This is my preferred recipe:

- 3 tbsp aloe vera gel
- 2 tbsp witch hazel
- ½ drop Vitamin E oil
- A few drops lemongrass essential oil (use lavender oil for children)
- A capful of (about 5 ml) BioPure Probiotic Concentrate diluted in 120 ml water

# TIP 20
## Use Natural Remedies for Baby's Minor Ailments

*Nature's treasure chest 2.0.*

### Teething

This commonly starts around the six months mark, although in rare cases babies are even born with teeth.[361] Again, there is a vast range of 'normal'. At this point, you will be relieved to find something which is safe enough to chew and helps your baby to relieve teething pain. What you don't want is your

---

361 https://www.nhs.uk/conditions/pregnancy-and-baby/teething-and-tooth-care/

Learn more about natural teething remedies at https://littlegreenfootpath.com/2019/07/20/natural-teething-remedies-the-top-6-options/

baby chewing away on some cheaply manufactured stuff, so it's best to be on the safe side. And before you reach for the Calpol,[362] try some natural and gentler remedies instead. I decided to go for a product which would be engaging for all five senses: touch, sight, sound, smell and taste. Lanco[363] produce toys made from one hundred per cent natural rubber collected from the Hevea tree (*Hevea brasiliensis*). The rubber is harvested without the use of herbicides as small slits are cut into the bark while the white sap, i.e. latex, is collected in cups, all of which is done by hand. Most of these toys are cute and painted with non-toxic, lead-free paints, and free from PVC, BPA and nitrosamines.[364] To clean them, use soapy water and a damp cloth, which is usually enough; you won't need to sterilise them.

If you want to go DIY, try a frozen banana, a wooden spoon or a frozen washcloth (wet and in the freezer for half an hour), which can all be helpful. You might also want to try a homeopathic remedy such as *Chamomilla* or *Pulsatilla*.[365]

Some mothers also swear by amber necklaces. Unfortunately, its effectiveness as a natural analgesic isn't entirely proven.[366] Nonetheless, the chewing alone will

---

362 https://www.independent.co.uk/life-style/teething-gel-warning-
    baby-stops-breathing-orajel-mother-facebook-viral-a8247611.html
363 https://www.lanco-toys.es/newborn
364 https://www.sciencedirect.com/topics/neuroscience/nitrosamines,
    https://www.bureauveritas.com/home/about-us/our-business/cps/
    whats-new/bulletins/cen-toy-safety-standard-nitrosamines and
    https://ec.europa.eu/health/ph_risk/committees/04_sccp/docs/
    sccp_q_148.pdf
365 https://www.homeopathycenter.org/teething
366 https://scienceornot.net/2012/10/30/amber-necklaces-and-
    teething-babies/

help, but then maybe opt for something safer as small beads can be swallowed all too easily.

## Cradle cap

Coconut oil works exceptionally well to cure this.[367] It has antifungal and antibacterial properties. Massage it onto the scalp and leave it on for a few minutes before you gently brush it off with a soft baby hairbrush, then wash your baby's hair with a gentle baby shampoo or wash, preferably non-fragrant.

## Blocked nose

Saline drops and a bulb syringe do the job just fine.[368] Do this to help your baby feed properly.

## Common colic

Frequent winding/burping should relieve this. In some cases, homeopathic remedies might do the trick.[369] Try a gentle tummy massage as well. Start at the navel and massage in a clockwise direction. Cycling your baby's legs

---

367 This is different from a fungal infection or a long-term skin condition called seborrhoeic dermatitis: http://www.bad.org.uk/shared/get-file.ashx?id=180&itemtype=document
Kokoso also sell a coconut oil scalp gel; have a look on their website, or try MooGoo Skincare: https://moogooskincare.co.uk/hair-and-scalp-care.html

368 https://www.babycenter.com/0_how-to-use-a-bulb-syringe-or-nasal-aspirator-to-clear-a-stuf_482.bc

369 https://www.homeopathycenter.org/homeopathy-today/natural-remedies-colic

in the air by gently holding onto their feet while they are lying on their back can also relieve trapped wind.

## *Nappy rash*

Before slathering on the antifungal steroid creams, include some more nappy-free time every day to prevent nappy rash in the first place. Go outside in the summer. Lie on a blanket and a towel to catch any accidents; and in the winter stay in front of the radiator or fire (with the necessary precautions) and stick on a pair of pants to go in the wash afterwards. Use Kokoso's coconut oil as a simple and additive-free nappy cream. And the best cure of them all: breast milk! Try and hand-express a few drops if you can, and rub it onto the affected area.

# TIP 21
## Choose a Good Vitamin Supplement to Suit Your and Your Baby's Needs

*The vitamin alphabet: A, B, K, C, D, E!*

### Who is this 'K'?

Even before your baby is born, you will be asked about the routine administration of Vitamin K directly after birth. Vitamin K is an agent necessary for normal blood clotting. It is now routinely administered to infants after birth, either as an injection or orally.[370] The latter will be done three times to ensure patient compliance as babies tend to spit out everything apart from milk.

---

370 https://www.ncbi.nlm.nih.gov/pmc/articles/PMC3021393/

The liver stores our lifelong Vitamin K supply. All we need is a tiny amount. Leafy green vegetables, cucumber, cheese, yoghurt and oils such as soya, rapeseed and olive contain one variety of this vitamin, identified as K1 and also known as phylloquinone, phytomenadione or phytonadione.[371] The other type, K2, also known as menaquinone or menatetrenone, is synthesised by certain intestinal bacteria, although there is an ongoing debate about its relevance for our needs.[372] In 2003 the American Academy of Pediatrics recommended that all neonates should receive Vitamin K1 as a single intramuscular dose of 0.5–1 mg. Doctors reaffirmed this recommendation in 2009.[373]

A lot of parents refuse this shot, thinking it is dangerous if the vitamin levels are brought up to high in their tiny infant's body as a result of the concentrated dose.[374] And so did I believing it wasn't necessary as long as the delivery had been relatively straightforward. The main reason was my desire to have as natural a birth as possible with as little intervention as possible, which is pretty much in line with the results of the American study cited above as to why parents refuse the shot. When I started writing this book, I did some more research into it and found out about some rather uncomfortable truths. Lack of Vitamin K in a neonate is a rare condition known as late haemorrhagic

---

371 https://www.ncbi.nlm.nih.gov/pmc/articles/PMC3021393/
372 https://www.ncbi.nlm.nih.gov/pubmed/1492156
373 https://www.ncbi.nlm.nih.gov/pmc/articles/PMC3021393/
374 https://www.ncbi.nlm.nih.gov/pmc/articles/PMC5526450/ – although this study is an American case study, the observation that vaccine refusal and those of other interventions are linked very much applies to other Western countries. A lot of it is fuelled by misinformation and half-truths which can often lead to confusion

disease of the newborn (HDN), which occurs in seventy in one hundred thousand births.[375] Contrary to my previously held belief, it does not seem to be linked with birth trauma such as ventouse or forceps deliveries, but it can happen to a perfectly healthy baby.[376] The reason for this kind of bleeding which can occur between eight days to 12 weeks or even six months after birth is owed to a lack of vitamin K prophylaxis and the fact that babies are born with insufficient stores of this vitamin.[377]

So, can we prevent this by supplementing with vitamins during pregnancy and while we are breastfeeding instead of the injection? In answer to this, another study aimed to evaluate the significance of antenatal supplementation of the mother with Vitamin K to augment her own stores to ensure some of it crossing the placenta to benefit the baby before birth as well as enriching the breastmilk to build up stores after birth. Although supplementation of the mother both before and after birth has been shown to have benefits, the study was weak in some points as it had to refer to old data and was unable to take social factors such as low-income families and dietary habits into account which may result in low Vitamin K levels in the mother.[378]

After all, it is still very much up to you if you feel that allowing this shot to be administered to your baby is against your principles. Personally, I have tried everything

---

375 https://www.ncbi.nlm.nih.gov/pubmed/16925960

376 https://evidencebasedbirth.com/evidence-for-the-vitamin-k-shot-in-newborns/ö; https://keepkidshealthy.com/2017/07/11/that-black-box-warning-on-vitamin-k-shots/

377 See previous footnote.

378 https://www.ncbi.nlm.nih.gov/pmc/articles/PMC6065418/

to achieve as natural a birth with as little intervention as possible (otherwise I wouldn't have sat down to write this book). However, in some cases we will need to reconsider and weigh up the available evidence. So, would I have consented to the administration of a dose of Vitamin K if I had known what I know now? Probably yes.

## The shining 'D'

Vitamin D is a fat-soluble vitamin, and is either synthesised subcutaneously by the human body through the action of sunlight or consumed as part of our diet via animal-based foods such as fatty fish, fish liver oil, and egg yolk.[379] Depending on its origin, Vitamin D can be identified as two physiologically different variants called D2 and D3. They have a similar metabolism in the human body which converts them into their active hormonal form.[380] Supplements contain both varieties of Vitamin D. The effect of your skin's melanin content on your capacity to absorb UV light in order to synthesise enough Vitamin D3 via your skin remains inconclusive, contrary to general opinion; however, some studies suggest an inverse correlation, i.e. the lighter your skin is, the less UV light you need to synthesise enough Vitamin D for your needs.[381] Vitamin D is also often described as crucial for a healthy pregnancy, but more research is needed to evaluate its role.[382] Sufficient Vitamin D is vital for the development of a healthy bone structure and nervous system.

---

379 https://www.ncbi.nlm.nih.gov/books/NBK56061/
380 https://www.ncbi.nlm.nih.gov/books/NBK56061/
381 https://www.ncbi.nlm.nih.gov/books/NBK56061/
382 https://www.ncbi.nlm.nih.gov/pmc/articles/PMC3747784/

Along with spending time outside in the sun, it makes sense to continue to take a vitamin supplement, especially for as long as you are breastfeeding. This also helps you to recuperate after the birth, and with the extra effort your body is making to produce nutritious breast milk.

## Fatty acids = faddy acids?

Long-chain omega-3 oils, also known by its scientific name docosahexaenoic acid (DHA), are derived from Norwegian fish or shellfish which should be sustainably sourced.[383] Omega-3 fats are proven to be beneficial to your baby's brain and eye development. It is therefore essential for you to ensure sufficient intake of these fatty acids during your pregnancy and while you are breastfeeding. If the thought does not sit well with you, for example, if you are vegetarian or vegan, you will need to replace them.[384] Vegetable oils such as flaxseed contain omega-3 fatty acids, but these are the short-chained variety, or alpha-linolenic acid (ALA). You would have to eat a lot to gain the same benefits you will get from DHA, but ALA is still a possible alternative if you are opposed to animal-based products – which is understandable because our oceans are soon likely to contain more plastic than fish.

---

383 https://www.vitabiotics.com/blogs/health-areas/the-beginner-s-guide-to-omega-3-fatty-acids; Vitabiotics source their fish from sustainable fisheries: https://www.vitabiotics.com/pages/ultra-fish-oil; to find out more: https://www.mcsuk.org/goodfishguide/search

384 You can find one of the vegan options at https://www.nothingfishy.co.uk

Sadly, our food is on the whole also less nutritious than it used to be, at least when produced by conventional methods.[385] When you choose a supplement, make sure it contains the right amount and balance of vitamins and minerals for your and your baby's needs.[386] Wild Nutrition is a good alternative if you want to go a bit less mainstream. They have products specifically designed for pregnant or breastfeeding women, and are different in that they use a so-called Food-Grown® process to manufacture their products.[387] You are supplementing with a nutritious food paste, which enables your body to absorb the nutrients more effectively as real, raw food.[388] You may also want to contact a medical herbalist[389] for tinctures and herbal teas to supplement your diet and support you and your baby.

# TIP 22
## Don't Be Afraid of Dirt

*Mud castles, here we come!*

Contrary to the Hygiene Hypothesis published in the 1980s,[390] we now know that controlled exposure to dirt

---

385 https://www.theguardian.com/lifeandstyle/2005/may/15/
foodanddrink.shopping3
386 Wild Nutrition (https://www.wildnutrition.com) offer free
consultation phone calls to find the right supplement for you.
387 https://www.wildnutrition.com/pages/food-grown-difference
388 https://www.wildnutrition.com/pages/why-our-supplements-are-
superior
389 https://www.nimh.org.uk/
390 https://www.ncbi.nlm.nih.gov/pmc/articles/PMC1448690/

can have beneficial effects.[391] According to a study at the University of Bristol, the so-called *Mycobacterium vaccae* found in soils can enhance our feeling of well-being.[392] The reason for this is the high level of the 'feel-good' hormone, serotonin. It is an equilibrium between benign bacteria and a healthy body which also enables the endocrine system to function correctly. Playing in the mud is thought to benefit the heart, skin and immune system, and have beneficial psychological effects such as increased happiness, reduced anxiety and enhanced learning.[393] According to J. F. Brody, the intuitive knowledge of this is inbuilt. Babies tend to suck their hands and "mouth" toys (and lots of other items lying about, as we all know!). This instinctive behaviour is crucial to help build up an immunity.[394] Dr Mary Ruebush, an American paediatrician, states that about 90 trillion microbes live on the human body at any one time.[395] I, for one, was far more afraid of my daughter ingesting synthetic fibres or microplastics than bits of dirt. While taking the necessary precautions, you won't need to disinfect everything as a little bit of dirt will most likely help your baby's immune system grow stronger.[396]

---

391 https://www.ncbi.nlm.nih.gov/pmc/articles/PMC4966430/
392 http://www.bristol.ac.uk/news/2007/11797584419.html
393 https://www.dirtisgood.com/home.html
394 http://www.wccc.ie/wp-content/uploads/2012/11/Dirt_Report_2012.pdf
395 M. Ruebush, *Why Dirt is Good: 5 Ways to Make Germs Your Friends* (2009).
396 See hand sanitiser recipe Tip 19.

# TIP 23
# Make an Informed Choice on Routine Vaccinations

*The science of immunity.*

## Wakefield and MMR

It all began with the infamous Wakefield study.[397] In 1998, Andrew Wakefield, a gastroenterologist, published his case series study in the renowned medical journal *The Lancet* in an article which has now long been retracted. He and twelve co-authors had studied twelve cases of the measles virus in the digestive systems of children who, after the measles, mumps and rubella (MMR) vaccine, began to exhibit symptoms of autism.[398] In the paper, the evidence had originally not been treated as conclusive enough to identify a causal relationship between MMR vaccination and autism. This changed after the broadcast of a video in which Wakefield suggested that the combined MMR vaccine should be suspended in favour of a series of three single-antigen vaccinations. He is thought to have made this statement after previously having filed for a patent for

---

397 https://www.historyofvaccines.org/content/articles/do-vaccines-cause-autism, https://www.nhs.uk/news/medication/no-link-between-mmr-and-autism-major-study-finds/, https://www.livescience.com/64909-measles-vaccine-not-linked-to-autism.html, https://adc.bmj.com/content/88/8/666 and https://www.autism.org.uk/get-involved/media-centre/position-statements/mmr-vaccine.aspx

398 Wakefield A, et al. (RETRACTED), 'Ileal-lymphoid-nodular hyperplasia, non-specific colitis, and pervasive developmental disorder in children' in *The Lancet* 1998, 351 (9103): 637–41.

these single-antigen vaccines. He therefore had a vested interest in promoting this approach.

An immediate panic followed after the news had been broadcast. It swept through newspapers, and terrified parents delayed or completely refused vaccination for their children, both in Britain and the United States. In Britain, MMR vaccination rates plummeted.[399]

Much research has been devoted to this issue since and the results have repeatedly shown there is no link between the MMR vaccine and autism. This includes a comprehensive review in 2014 of all available studies on links between autism and vaccines, using data from more than 1.25 million children.[400]

In addition, the original research linking the MMR vaccine and autism has been comprehensively discredited. All of this resulted in Wakefield being struck from the medical register.[401]

## Responsible decisions

According to the accepted theory, injecting a strand of bacteria (either live or non-live)[402] will help the body combat the infection should it come into contact with it later as it has already built up some targeted antibodies. Contrary to that, sceptics argue that a lot of the diseases once rampant in Europe and North America have been eradicated thanks to an improvement in living conditions and better nutrition, and not because of routine

399 P. A. Offit, *Autism's False Profits* 2008, Chapters 2 and 3.
400 http://www.sciencedirect.com/science/article/pii/ S0264410X14006367?np=y
401 http://news.bbc.co.uk/1/hi/health/8695267.stm
402 https://www.vaccines.gov/basics/types/index.html

immunisation.[403] One has to bear in mind, however, that we are judging the present situation from the narrow perspective of highly industrialised nations. We are used to a very high level of so-called 'herd immunity' amongst the general population, which is historically speaking quite exceptional. The extent of this public immunity still varies a lot elsewhere in the world.[404] And that is the whole point: immunologically speaking we are suffering from a blackout, meaning we don't really know what it used to be like before, and it is a little bit like imagining a world without antibiotics. Because we have such a high ratio of immunity, we are allowed the luxury of choice. Just consider this: a recent report has shown how measles cases are soaring in the US.[405] There were more cases during the first half of 2019 than during any full year since 2006, according to a report by the World Health Organization.[406]

Looking at the evidence, that is exactly why I decided to have my daughter immunised against meningitis, polio and MMR because I thought it vital in those particular cases. Despite all that, it may still be beneficial to look into the vaccination programme carefully and not rely solely on the government's recommendations.[407] I did, for example, refuse the BCG (tuberculosis) vaccine, which she was offered as soon as I mentioned that I was born in Indonesia. I looked into it carefully and discussed it

403 https://avn.org.au/
404 https://www.nhs.uk/conditions/travel-vaccinations/
405 https://www.newyorker.com/magazine/2019/09/02/the-message-of-measles
406 https://www.who.int/immunization/diseases/measles/en/
407 https://www.vaccines.gov/basics/work/prevention/index.html

with various other health professionals and my husband, gathering information and different opinions, before I came to the conclusion that I did not want to subject her to any more stress, which a very potent vaccine such as BCG is likely to cause. I also figured that where we live the risk is very low; neither were we planning to travel to Indonesia or other high-risk countries, nor did we have any relatives still resident there who could potentially carry the disease. I also had some tuberculin antibodies in my blood as it had been recorded by a paediatrician in my immunisation booklet back in the 1980s. From my personal point of view, one should not be swayed by a default reaction to accept everything uncritically only because it is recommended. On the other hand, we shouldn't automatically assume that the medical-industrial complex and all their advice is by necessity bad. So, even though it is a lot to ask of parents to make this critical decision all alone, it is probably best to try and talk to different people about it, and gather different opinions and viewpoints.[408]

Considering rising antibiotic resistance,[409] it is vital to build up the body's overall protection. Any of the illnesses or diseases commonly vaccinated against can be debilitating, and life-changing once contracted, but in cases of previous immunisation, the symptoms are at least usually milder.[410] It also depends on your travel plans as even if one is at a low risk at home, that might

---

408 https://www.informedparent.co.uk/ offers an interesting resource for an alternative take on that.

409 http://www.who.int/news-room/fact-sheets/detail/antibiotic-resistance

410 https://www.vaccines.gov/basics/work/prevention/index.html

not be the case when travelling abroad. These are all facts which need to be taken into account when making your choice. There is, of course, a lot you can do for your child's health besides, such as eating healthy foods and spending lots of time with them, and spending time outdoors in an environment which should be as natural as possible.

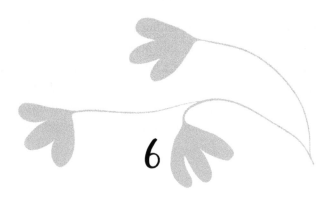

# 6

# A Greener Home

## TIP 24
### Reduce the Use of Chemicals at Home

*Fresh breeze without Febreze.*

If you think it a good idea to start reducing your exposure to harmful chemicals when it comes to your toiletries, the same certainly applies to your cleaning products and furnishings in your home. Think of synthetic fragrances such as plug-in air fresheners, and many of the types of floorings and paints we use in our homes. We mostly assume that there is very little we can do about it and that we have no choice. But we do! Just let me run you through some of the principal points.

Despite statistics[411] providing some evidence that the air quality outside has quite literally gone out the window in recent years, it is best to regularly open your windows

---

411 https://www.bbc.co.uk/news/health-43964341

and perhaps even sleep with them partially open, although this might be a safety issue depending on where you live. Circulating the air is the best way to prevent the build-up of mould in bathrooms and lingering smells like stale cooking odours in your home. There is perhaps even an issue with insulation leading to a build-up of humidity, and hence mould,[412] although the benefits seem to outweigh the problems as it is to date probably the most energy-efficient route to a temperate home.

But there are little steps you can take to improve your indoor air. Ditch the air spray and anything you have to plug in. The latter also come in ridiculous amounts of packaging and contain VOCs.[413] The air-freshener Febreze was evaluated in 2009 by the Environmental Working Group (EWG).[414] Their results showed that the product (in the Hawaiian Aloha fragrance) released eighty-nine air contaminants, including one carcinogen. On the label, some vague names and descriptions of various ingredients appear, such as odour eliminator, fragrance, non-flammable natural propellant, and quality control ingredients.

The EWG looked into these ingredients further and found:

- ACETALDEHYDE: This is on California's Proposition 65 list for cancer and reproductive toxicity.
- ETHYL ACETATE: A chemical toxic to the brain and nervous system.

---

412 https://www.nuaire.co.uk/news/residential/indoor-air-quality-the-next-big-issue
413 https://en.wikipedia.org/wiki/Volatile_organic_compound
414 https://www.ewg.org/

- BUTYLATED HYDROXYTOLUENE (BHT): Linked with neurotoxicity, hormone disruption, allergies, and irritation to the skin, eyes or lungs.
- PROPYLENE GLYCOL: Linked with allergies and skin and eye irritation.
- 1,3-DICHLORO-2-PROPANOL[415]: A chemical also used in flame retardants, resins, plastics and rubber. It has been linked with cancer in animal studies, according to the California Environmental Protection Agency.[416]

After the National Resources Defense Council (NRDC) in the USA[417] had tested fourteen different air fresheners in 2007, including Febreze, they were able to find that they contained phthalates, which can affect our endocrine systems and have been linked with childhood asthma.[418]

If and when possible, get rid of carpeting and linoleum flooring and choose paints and varnishing for your floors that are certified, i.e. have an EU Ecolabel.[419] The main sources of human-made VOCs in homes are lurking in paints and protective coatings. Typical solvents are aliphatic hydrocarbons,[420] ethyl acetate,[421]

---

415 https://pubchem.ncbi.nlm.nih.gov/compound/1%2C3-dichloro-2-propanol

416 https://calepa.ca.gov/

417 https://www.nrdc.org/

418 https://cvskinlabs.com/phthalates-linked-with-childhood-asthma-and-many-other-health-problems/

419 https://ec.europa.eu/environment/ecolabel/

420 https://www.thoughtco.com/definition-of-aliphatic-hydrocarbon-604763

421 https://en.wikipedia.org/wiki/Ethyl_acetate

glycol ethers, and acetone.[422] Fortunately, motivated by cost, environmental concerns, and regulation, the paint and coating industries are increasingly shifting toward aqueous solvents.[423]

To freshen up your indoor air naturally, you can make potpourri according to the season, such as lavender sachets in summer, and orange and cloves for Christmas.

## *Lavender sachets*

Fill small see-through muslin sachets with fresh lavender and place them around the house. Bruise the flowers a bit to help them give off their fragrance.

## *Orange and clove potpourri*

Tie a cute ribbon around an orange, cross it over once and bring it back, so that you can see four quarters of orange peel. Stick a whole bunch of cloves into the orange, perhaps making a pattern, and display it in your living room.

# TIP 25
## Make Your Own Household Cleaning Agents

*Magic cauldron!*

Using chemical detergents in your home can have a devastating effect not only on your and your children's

---

422 https://en.wikipedia.org/wiki/Acetone
423 https://en.wikipedia.org/wiki/Aqueous_solution

health,[424] but also on wildlife as it gets into our water systems. The effectiveness of conventional washing-up liquid in reducing the surface tension of water pollutes rivers and lakes and destroys the mucus layer of fish.[425] Petrochemically derived detergents also contain optical whiteners which can cause skin irritation, especially on babies' delicate skin.

Making your own cleaning agents can turn into an interesting hobby and isn't as time-consuming as you might think. From as little as about five ingredients, you can make most cleaning agents and will be able to keep your house tidy and clean-smelling. Very often these ingredients can also be used on their own. It is not only safer and healthier for your home, and therefore your baby, but also better for the environment and ultimately your budget.

For a basic kit to get you started on your DIY journey, you will need white vinegar, bicarbonate of soda, washing soda, citric acid, borax substitute and curd soap.[426] Household salt and vegetable starch (such as potato starch) will also be invaluable to mix some of the cleaning agents. Use essential oils to add nice smells and enhance their disinfectant properties.

To wipe kitchen worktops and tables and to do the inevitable dusting, invest in an E-Cloth[427]. This is a brilliant

---

424 http://www.mescoursespourlaplanete.com/medias/all/res_ngfa2d.pdf

425 https://www.lenntech.com/aquatic/detergents.htm and https://www.ncbi.nlm.nih.gov/pmc/articles/PMC4264028/

426 https://littlegreenfootpath.com/resources-2/
Also have a look at Wendy Graham's blog Moral Fibres (https://moralfibres.co.uk/) and her book *Fresh Clean Home* (https://moralfibres.co.uk/fresh-clean-home/).

427 https://www.e-cloth.com/

innovation that enables you to use a microfibre cloth with just water. You can add a splash of vinegar and put it in a spray bottle. Just wet the cloth with a couple of squirts.

Combat dust mites by vacuuming your beds regularly and washing your bedding, as well as keeping the heating low and investing in a dehumidifier or air purifier.[428]

For your laundry, try either more eco-friendly products or Ecoballs, which release ionised oxygen which lifts dirt from fabric.[429] The only downside to them is that they are yet another product made from plastic, even though they are not single-use plastic, which we'd like to avoid if we can possibly help it. You can also make your detergent based on RSPO[430] certified curd soap.[431] And last but not least, soap nut shells[432] are an extremely versatile natural product which are absolutely zero waste! They can be used for up to five times to wash your laundry. Add between five and eight shells into a small cotton bag that comes as part of the delivery and add it directly to your laundry in the drum. Soap nuts can also be boiled to make a liquid detergent. After you have used them several times to wash your clothes or to make your laundry detergent, the exhausted nuts are still good for your garden as a fertiliser or pest repellent. The liquid soap can also be used

---

428 https://littlegreenfootpath.com/2018/08/25/a-fresh-breeze-without-febreze/
   For mattresses go to Tip 9.
429 https://en.wikipedia.org/wiki/Laundry_ball and https://ecozone.com/products/ecozone-ecoballs/
430 https://rspo.org/
431 These are just a few examples. For more resources, visit my blog https://littlegreenfootpath.com and sites such as https://brendid.com, https://moralfibres.co.uk and https://www.smarticular.net/en
432 https://www.soapnuts.co.uk/

as a multi-purpose cleaner or pest repellent spray for your house plants, or put them in a blender with about 500 ml of water to make a foam wash which can be used to wash dishes, your dog or even yourself and the kids (well, not the baby, perhaps!).

It is perhaps a good idea to keep some products such as Sonett or Bio-D as a backup should you run out of your home-made ones. These are also a good alternative if you are not too keen on making cleaning products yourself. And consider getting a Guppyfriend.[433] Every time we wash our clothes, countless plastic fibres from synthetic textiles are washed into rivers and oceans. The Guppyfriend washbag has been specially designed with micro-filter materials to catch the tiniest microfibres released from textiles during a wash cycle. It has been scientifically approved and patented to reduce microplastics. You will still need to collect the fibres and dispose of them after the wash cycle.

# TIP 26
# Reduce Packaging (Especially Plastics)

*Jack in the box.*

Have you ever realised how absurd it is to spend money on things you are just going to throw away? However, that is exactly what we are doing daily, reaching a peak around Christmastime, birthdays and other celebrations. Think about reducing the amount of single-use plastic waste you are creating. Why not try and make your wrapping paper from recyclable paper and decorate it with dried leaves?

---

433 http://guppyfriend.com/en/

Use cloth wipes instead of disposable wipes. Limit your use of disposable wipes to when you are out and about. Ask yourself: why would you spend good money on something which isn't much more than toilet paper and water? Most of them also contain plastic fibres to make them more durable, although there are some notable exceptions.[434]

If you are ordering from online stores, try retailers such as &Keep[435] or Ecco Verde[436] as they minimise the use of plastic in their packaging. Look out for companies such as Natural Rubber Toys (formerly Mushroom & Co.)[437], who not only use 100% natural rubber and food-grade dyes to produce their toys but also recycled paper packaging when they send them out to you or display them in shops.

Also, stop using single-use plastic bags, perhaps even altogether, and get your bag for life instead. You can carry a fold-up one in your rucksack or handbag. And ditch the cling film. Use storage containers instead, or just use a Pyrex bowl with a plate on top. Recycle old glass jars. Try and buy loose fruit and veggies as much as you can, and avoid wrapping them in a small plastic bag which will then go in yet another plastic bag. It all seems like tiny steps, but we have got to start somewhere to make a change![438]

---

434 https://www.independent.co.uk/extras/indybest/fashion-beauty/make-up/best-face-wipes-biodegradable-eco-friendly-make-up-removal-a7535016.html

435 https://andkeep.com/

436 https://www.ecco-verde.co.uk/

437 https://www.naturalrubbertoys.co.uk/

438 I'll go into this in more detail in my next book, *A Green Home Life*. Also, have a look at my blog (https://littlegreenfootpath.com) for updates.

# 7

# Play to Learn –
# and Learn to Play

Executive function and your baby's development:[439]
a shortcut to what a baby is 'supposed'
to be doing (or not!)

ncluding a section about education and learning in a book about a 'greener' approach to parenting your baby may seem a bit ambitious or weird or both – and yet, people even try to 'teach' foreign languages to their unborn babies.[440] I am not saying that this is good or bad. I believe that learning, especially when it comes to babies, is and should by necessity be a long way away from regulated teaching, which again is different from implementing regularity in your child's day and week. Routines are essential in many ways, but so is the freedom

---

439 https://www.frontiersin.org/articles/10.3389/fpsyg.2014.00593/full
440https://www.livestrong.com/article/161114-how-to-teach-a-baby-
in-the-womb/

to roam, discover and explore, and both go hand in hand. This section is, therefore, very much about a mix between guidance and unguided play and exploration.

Our babies are experts – and there are none better. They are born with a mind-boggling capacity to learn, absorbing everything like a sponge. To begin with, it is all preverbal; they learn through their emotions. They do it all themselves if we provide the right environment and are there to protect and nurture them while they discover and explore. They need loving, personal interaction as their first step of learning. As they begin to understand that they are safe and you are reliable as a parent, they will start to develop healthy relationships with themselves and future teachers or tutors. Lev Vygotsky identified actual relationships as the origin of all higher cognitive functions.[441]

Psychologists distinguish between three primary faculties which are the foundation for healthy cognitive development, also known as executive function.[442] The term 'executive function' refers to an interrelated set of mental processes whose three primary dimensions are memory, self-control and mental flexibility. The faculty of memory enables us to retain information to complete tasks. Self-control facilitates us, in our interactions with others, to make considered responses instead of giving in to impulses. Mental flexibility is essential for us to respond appropriately to different situations.

For the development of these skills, the years between birth and five are critical. During that time, the

---

441 https://www.instructionaldesign.org/theories/social-development/
442 https://developingchild.harvard.edu/science/key-concepts/
  executive-function/

foundations of brain circuits are laid out. For babies, all this starts with responsive interaction, i.e. not letting them 'cry it out' etc. They need a sense of secure attachment for their healthy emotional and social development, both closely intertwined with cognitive function. Although these abilities come into effect later in life than the stage we are looking at in this book, the foundations for a child's unimpeded development begin at an early age. These are also the foundation for additional skills such as emotional control, initiative, planning and organisation. A daily routine simply means repeating the same activity at roughly the same time and in a recognisable way. A familiar daily pattern will help your child to feel secure. For babies, this applies to any activity performed in close proximity to them. They react to familiar voices, your face and hands, and colours and geometric shapes in books, on soft cubes, mobiles or patterns on textiles. Ultimately, it is about being a sociable and happy person, which is what most parents want for their child. But how can getting your child out into natural surroundings be helpful in this respect?

Usual suggestions of play appropriate for young babies can be enhanced through experiencing beauty, peace and wonder outside. Lap games, peek-a-boo, rhyming games and body part games, which all help to develop memory and necessary self-control, also work wonderfully in an outside setting. Access to nature can help with calming a fussy baby or a frazzled parent. You can cherish these special moments of quiet bonding in the fresh air, the warmth of the sun and perhaps a gentle breeze. It is more about being there, not getting there, as nature is everywhere. Embrace the elements and model curiosity;

bring friends if you like, and create stories. Along with all the other aspects this book touches on, this will hopefully be part of a stable and mature relationship.

# TIP 27
## Buy or Find Natural Toys

*The inner child…*

*Indeed, so powerful are the metaphorical gender cues that five-year-old children will confidently declare that a spiky brown tea set and an angry-looking baby doll dressed in rough black clothing are for boys, while a smiling yellow truck adorned with hearties and a yellow hammer strewn with ribbons are for girls.*

Cordelia Fine, *The Gender Delusion*

Before you buy toys for your baby (or your older children, for that matter), you might want to consider the following questions:

- What material is used to make my baby's toys?
- Where have they been made?
- Who has made them?

As a simple guideline, it makes sense to look for toys that won't break too soon, which a lot of the cheaply manufactured toys do pretty quickly. Most of the time, they don't leave much room for imagination either. The other two questions are of a more environmental and ethical nature. We need to think about sustainable manufacture and whether those who make the toys receive a fair wage for the work they do so our kids can enjoy themselves. And, on another note, for how long is your child going to play with their toys? Are they of such good quality that they can maybe even be passed on to siblings or friends, or donated to a playgroup or nursery?

One of the brands to look out for in toy shops is PlanToys.[443] They make beautiful, ethically and sustainably manufactured wooden toys, which are of educational benefit too. The trees that provide the wood for this fabulous range of toys are harvested carefully and sustainably. Initially, they are used to produce rubber, and once they have stopped doing that, they are cut down and then taken to the factory to make toys. The wood is kiln-dried, and non-formaldehyde glue and water-based dyes are used. Even the packaging has been recycled. Physical, social, emotional, intellectual and language skills are all supported as well as imaginative play. Small soft toys which aren't too big for babies' hands and are made from organic cotton are also good.[444] If you can, try and find a toy shop in your area that sells these types of toys. Have a look at the directory at the end of this book to find out more about sustainably and ethically produced toys.

## Natural toys vs gender stereotyping

Also, right from the start try and avoid limiting your child's interests by giving in to gender stereotyping. Whenever this topic comes up in a group setting, people very quickly

---

443 http://www.plantoys.com/
444 http://lettoysbetoys.org.uk/early-learning-let-toys-be-toys-gift-guide-2/#more-7964

split into two camps, and you will almost inevitably hear one of the parents say, "Well, I tried all the boys' toys with my girl, but she still wants to be the princess dressed up in pink." This statement is very often followed by a shrug and sometimes even a sigh.

Let's have a look at the sentence again: *boys'* toys? Well, that is the problem right there. They did not say just 'toys', did they? The item, whatever it was, had already been labelled before Daughter X even started playing with it. It would be like saying to you, "Never mind, just wear your husband's T-shirt and trainers. You don't like them? Your friends think it's funny? You've got to understand, sweetheart, it is a statement. Are you still with me?" I am being really facetious here and only unintentionally patronising, but let's rewind this: we want toys without labels. We want toys suitable for anybody, be they boy or girl.

The actual problem, in my view, does not reflect girls' genetic hardwiring which they cannot escape ('I must be Snow White/Sleeping Beauty/Cinderella' Syndrome), but firstly the mind-boggling masses of 'stuff' that lure even the youngest of children into active consumerism, and secondly (and more importantly) the way children identify with their peers. If a girl feels that she is indeed a girl, why would she want to play with her brother's toys if her friends wouldn't? The point is not that the toys are unsuitable as such, but that the girl is subliminally made to feel that they are and that she'll be ridiculed[445] if she plays with them. It seems like a difficult cycle to break.

---

445 http://lettoysbetoys.org.uk/bullying-the-role-of-gender-based-marketing/

But what does all of this have to do with going green? One aspect, certainly, is that we do not deem toys suitable to be passed on to younger siblings[446] if they are of the opposite sex. Another point is that this system countermands social justice and equality. And that is probably central to the problem. The following image emerges: society is divided into two (and strangely enough only two) types of people – one active and aggressive; the other quiet and caring.[447] Did we not move on from that? These stereotypical images reverberate into adulthood and are directly linked to the choices people make in later life, like the gender pay gap, and women turning out to be easy targets for the cosmetics and diet industries.[448]

For some time, campaigns have been run[449] to urge manufacturers and retailers to curb the stereotyping, which is, as indicated in the *Ask the expert* box below, very much a marketing ploy.[450] Despite divided opinions, we have to see it for what it is: a cultural label, not inherent genetic programming that will unfold as the child grows up unable to resist its powerful pull, and which makes one sex ill-suited and the other fit for a particular purpose.[451]

---

446 https://www.theguardian.com/lifeandstyle/2014/apr/22/gendered-toys-stereotypes-boy-girl-segregation-equality

447 http://lettoysbetoys.org.uk/raising-children-without-gender-stereotypes/#more-7801

448 https://www.cteg.org.uk/wp-content/uploads/2017/07/Gendered-toys-Final-report-Alice-Mc-Neill.pdf

449 http://lettoysbetoys.org.uk/, or follow them on Twitter: https://twitter.com/LetToysBeToys

450 https://www.theguardian.com/lifeandstyle/2014/apr/22/gendered-toys-stereotypes-boy-girl-segregation-equality

451 https://www.andrews.edu/~rbailey/Chapter%20one/9040385.pdf

It is based on what we believe according to cultural convention, and this is very powerful indeed.

# TIP 28

## Provide a Gentle and Natural Playtime for Your Baby[452]

*Toy foraging!*

Making and finding your toys can be as easy as using a stick or a cotton ball or a sock. Be creative! Imagine what simple things can turn into, how a folded piece of paper could metamorphose into a bird, or a leaf shape-shift into a boat.

You can use your voice, face and hands as toys. Keep talking to your baby and vary your facial expression. Smile, frown, purse your lips, look happy, thoughtful and surprised.[453]

You can make soft pom-pom balls; patchwork cubes you sew together from oddments of fabric and fill up with soft material, like fabric scraps. Or you can sew a rag book or make a mobile. Make your mobile from unwanted CDs or DVDs. Most of us should still have some of them hanging about. They reflect the light beautifully when hung up in a window. Cards with geometric patterns work very well too. In fact, geometric shapes and a baby's interest in

---

452 For more ideas visit https://laughingkidslearn.com, https:// mamasmiles.com, https://simpleplayideas.com and https:// nurturestore.co.uk, and read *Playtime* by Elspeth and Fiona Richards (see Recommended Reading).

453 E. and F. Richards, *Playtime* (2010), loc. 176ff.

them are perhaps the first glimpse of a mathematical mind. With toddlers, this becomes more apparent when they are stacking toys or sorting shapes. It all starts with geometry and realising simple relations between things, such as "*this thing is bigger than this one*". You can also count rubber ducks in the bath, count the number of steps when going up the stairs, or use nursery rhymes with numbers (see Tip 30).

You can paint pebbles as well, but make sure your baby cannot swallow them. You can use baskets, wooden chests or cloth bags to store toys instead of plastic boxes. If you have already got them, by all means use them (so do I), but don't buy any new ones. Non-plastic containers usually last a lot longer and are easier to recycle, such as wicker baskets. You might also take to the idea of making a sensory treasure bag for your baby. That way they can touch things of different textures. You could include items such as a natural sponge, a pastry brush, a wooden spoon, soft and shiny pieces of cloth, and a pine cone.

Toys don't need to be expensive. When your baby is a little older, they will most likely enjoy playing the drums with saucepans. You won't need a battery-powered plastic xylophone to entertain them.[454]

As your baby becomes more responsive, they are bound to love hiding games. According to Elspeth and Fiona Richards,[455] variations like hiding your face behind

---

454 Clean bath toys with vinegar and make sure they are PVC-, BPA- and phthalate free. Invest in a natural rubber duck (https://www.babipur.co.uk/real-rubber-duck-natural.html; https://www.greentulip.co.uk/baby-and-child/baby-toys-and-comforters/small-duck-yellow.html; https://heveaplanet.com/shop/kawan/).

455 Read more about simple games and capturing babies' attention in their book *Playtime* (2010).

your hands and pulling them away to say, "Boo!" or "Peek-a-boo!", or hiding toys underneath a piece of cloth or a blanket and uncovering them again work very well. They also suggest you encourage your baby to imitate you by repeating words often, such as "Dad, Dad, Dad" or "Mum, Mum, Mum."[456]

I always feel it is best to make your baby feel that they are part of your life and what you are doing. Try and adapt whatever it is that needs to be done around the house and let them repeat the same activity over and over again until they feel that they have mastered it. Even going for a walk and looking at leaves rustling in the wind can be considered play. It is all to do with exploration and not too much artificial stimulation. Be led by your baby in this respect. You can also turn baby massage into a game and accompany this with rhymes or singing.[457] 'This Little Piggy' works very well while providing sensory experience. It is the first step in helping them to get to know their body. You can start with a baby massage routine when your baby is about six weeks old.[458] It is also a relaxing part of a bedtime routine. The recommendation for a bedtime routine is to start implementing one from about three months.[459] I personally think we should still try and be flexible for our own and our babies' sake. Most of these routines will probably take some time to become

---

456 Elspeth and Fiona Richards, *Playtime* (2010) loc. 178f..

457 Also look on https://iaim.org.uk for more information, and in M. Corkhill, *Green Parenting* (2006), 37.

458 https://www.nct.org.uk/baby-toddler/everyday-care/baby-massage-tips-and-benefits

459 https://www.nhs.uk/conditions/pregnancy-and-baby/getting-baby-to-sleep/

effective at such a young age. Your baby may sleep through the night from nine weeks old or they may still be waking at least twice by the time they are two years old. Try not to give in to our culture's obsession with sleep training and getting babies to sleep through the night (go back to Tip 4 to find out why). The best way is to make your routine as gentle and playful as possible.

# Ask the expert: Ken Goode, proprietor of Jenny Wren Toys in Castle Douglas, Dumfries and Galloway

King Street in Castle Douglas is a typical Scottish high street. As you walk along, you will find an inconspicuous-looking toy shop, tucked in between M&Co clothing and the surgery office of a local councillor. This impression changes, though, once you go through the door, as Jenny Wren Toys is so unlike most other toy shops. You won't find any toy guns (which is an oxymoron anyway). There are no Barbie dolls or My Little Ponies. There is almost no plastic to be seen. Ken Goode, who runs the shop, has a background in education. It is his vision to make parenting and education more natural and sustainable, less prone to marketing ploys and free from gender bias, while aiming to facilitate a playful and therefore enjoyable approach to learning. Let's see what he has to say about toys and their pivotal role in bringing up our children.

*How does sustainability work with toys?*

Sustainability works on three levels. It starts with the design of the toy, the materials used to make it, and the actual manufacturing process. If you take PlanToys and Lanka Kade as examples, they are also ensuring an ethical manufacturing process. The design ensures that they won't break easily, nothing can snap off, so durability is a feature. In my own family, my son and daughter-in-law have three children, and a toy that once belonged to the eldest, who is ten, has been passed on to the youngest, who is fourteen months. And these toys are also fun, which toys should be. As for the materials used, wood gives, in my personal view, a better tactile experience than plastic, so it enables children to engage with natural material. These can either be moulded, as in PlanToys' case, or solid wood, as in Lanka Kade's case. The wooden animals from the Lanka Kade range are also decorated with water-based paints.

*During your time in the shop, have you seen any changes in customer behaviour and demand?*

We have been running the shop for eight years, and in that time there have been some changes. It is more difficult to source these kinds of toys, for a start. If you take Fisher-Price, for example, you can see that the market for these toys is not children, but adults, who falsely think that these are the kinds of toys children would like, until they find out that all these toys do is make lots of noise and neither have they been made to last. I once had to buy some batteries for a plastic crane of my grandson's which cost me £11 and the batteries lasted for two days. There is no sustainability involved, and it just creates waste. Unfortunately, it has become harder over time to source alternatives, and the choice of sustainable toys has been reduced.

*What are your main aims as regards sustainability and the reduction of packaging?*

We aim to provide high quality and durability. The same applies to packaging. The boxes for PlanToys are all made in the same straightforward design without a display window and just a simple wrapping paper inside. There is no plastic frame you will need to cut open with a pair of scissors. A picture on the outside indicates what is inside. The simplicity of it means I can take the item out and display it without damaging the box too much and easily put it back in when I sell it. We do sell plastic toys. There is WOW toys[460], for example. What is different here is that they are BPA- and PVC-free, they do not use toxic paint and are more durable. WOW has also stopped using plastic windows in their packaging; the boxes are open now. We are a small shop, and in bigger ones where it is more difficult to personally interact with customers in the way we do, they want to prevent customers from touching and potentially damaging toys.

*How do you circumvent the 'gender trap'?*

First of all, we do not have clear departments in the shop. We try and mix up toys as much as possible. In a lot of shops, items would be displayed in a boy window and a girl window – one is blue, the other is pink. To illustrate how deeply ingrained this is, I had a grandmother come in who wanted a soft toy, a bunny, for her grandson. I said, "Here we go, here's a bunny." And she said, "Oh no, it's for a girl." She did not buy the rabbit because the insides of its ears were pink. She wanted blue.

---

460 https://wowtoys.com/

Gender stereotyping is mostly a marketing ploy. I used to buy these wooden bikes in red. The company I worked with stopped making them in red and white. They are now in pink and blue, which means I would have to buy double the amount because some will exclusively buy pink and some blue. There is a big dichotomy going on. It is not in the genes.

*So, would you say that one of the educational benefits of play is imagination?*

Yes, absolutely. I once had somebody look for a toy animal, a fox or an elephant. I got out one of the Lanka Kade[461] wooden animals, beautifully painted. I got asked by the customer who wanted it for her grandson, "What does it do?" She probably expected you would need to switch it on somewhere for it make a sound or start moving. My answer was, "You can make them what you want them to do. If you want it to run it runs. If you want it to make sounds, you are free to pretend that it does. If you want it to eat or sleep or hide, you can do that." The whole conversation I have just described is probably symptomatic of the 'whizz-bangery' we are so used to now. We need to help our children to use their imagination instead and be inventive in their play. Conceptual development is also about acquiring gross and fine motor skills, and sharing, which comes later on at about three to four years. It is a shift in the concept of self, facilitated through play.

---

461 https://www.lankakade.co.uk/

# TIP 29
## Sing Rather than Play Music from the Computer or Phone

*Nightingale with some orchestral support.*

Your baby loves the sound of your voice; it's their favourite, even if you think you can't sing. Even babies as young as two or three months old will benefit from hearing you sing. Sing lullabies at night while you rock your baby gently in your arms. Don't be afraid to be out of tune. It's a beautiful thing to do when you are starting to establish a bedtime routine. You can also use a soft lullaby toy with a little music box inside which plays your favourite tune as you pull on a string. I found it helped very much with the singing.

Sing at other times as well. This works well while incorporating some very gentle movement of baby's limbs. Hold their feet and do a gentle cycling movement with their legs. This is also a good time to start attending music groups with your little one. Your baby is likely to enjoy the playful approach to rhythm and language. The company of other babies and children comes as a bonus.

The NHS give out leaflets with lots of play ideas and some nursery rhymes. Get a book from the library or look some of the songs up online if you are a bit rusty. I thought it was rather fun to learn some of the old rhymes and find out about their origins.[462]

---

462 https://www.historic-uk.com/CultureUK/More-Nursery-Rhymes/

# TIP 30

## Go to Playgroups where they Teach Nursery Rhymes and Read Stories from Books

*If you're happy and you know it...*

Try and find out about what's on at your local library. Even if some sessions seem repetitive to you, your baby will learn playfully by repetition and association to form a repertoire to last throughout their life. Some easy rhymes your baby is most likely going to enjoy from very early on are 'Baa, Baa, Black Sheep' and 'Row, Row, Row Your Boat', and little finger games like 'This Little Piggy' and 'Round and Round the Garden'. As they get older, your baby will also enjoy simple action rhymes and peek-a-boo. So, it's a perfect opportunity for you to learn a few more rhymes yourself and maybe also get to know other parents. Your health visitor will usually give out a list of suitable groups in your area.

# TIP 31

## Look at Picture Books Featuring Plants and Animals Together

*The great menagerie 1.0.*

Despite all the things available online, such as videos and e-books, there is nothing like the tactile experience of turning a page which is a skill that is starting to be lost in the age of touchscreens.[463] There is another good reason to make use of your local library. That way, you won't need to buy the books all at once. Also, you might not always want to go for the books targeted explicitly at babies or very young children. Vary the things you show to your baby, although very soon they are probably going to acquire a favourite which will have to be read out to them over and over and over again! About halfway through baby's first year, they are likely to show more interest in books, albeit that their attention span is still short. Replicate the sounds different animals make. Point them out time and time again. Enjoy the colours and give brief explanations. Try and find out what your baby likes best.

# TIP 32
## Watch Nature Programmes

*Amateur biologist!*

Even in her earliest days, I had my daughter listen to David Attenborough's voice from time to time. His BBC series *Blue Planet* and *Life* are engaging programmes for you and your baby to watch together. This can help to increase your own knowledge so you can answer their questions as they grow up. Sure, there is always Google, but how much more impressive if we are able to use our brain for one of its most brilliant faculties, i.e. to retain and access information!

---

463 https://inews.co.uk/culture/books/children-are-picking-up-books-and-trying-to-swipe-left-teachers-told-as-concern-for-future-of-local-libraries-grows-512289

On another note, nature programmes provide one of the many ways to inspire love and awe for the natural world and our place in it. From very early on, we will have to teach our children about the dangerous effects that an economic system geared towards continuous growth has on the resources of our planet and the other species who share it with us.[464] What better way to do that than to immerse ourselves in the wonder and beauty of our home planet – even if it's on-screen from time to time?

---

464 This article looks into the problem of trying to decouple GDP growth from its adverse environmental impact. It conclusively argues that economic growth is a poor proxy for societal well-being, and that alternatives to GDP growth as a favourable goal will need to be found to make our economies more sustainable: https://journals.plos.org/plosone/article?id=10.1371/journal.pone.0164733

# 8

# Outdoors with Baby

*We live at a time when extraordinary learning resources*
*are available for schools everywhere. We are on the threshold*
*of deeper planetary awareness, an emerging understanding*
*of biosphere dynamics, a comprehensive "science of*
*integration". But none of this will occur without challenging*
*the status quo of science education. We should be planning*
*schools to train a Gaian generation of learners, students who*
*see the biosphere in every habitat and organism, who are*
*equipped to interpret environmental change, who are keen*
*to observe the natural world, and who know that their very*
*survival may depend on it.*

Mitchell Thomashow, 'The Gaian Generation: A New
Approach to Environmental Learning' in *Gaia in*
*Turmoil*, edited by Eileen Crist and H. Bruce Rinker

This chapter contains a lot of tips and ideas on how to facilitate access to nature. In wanting to protect our children from harm, we have probably – with the best of intentions – condemned them to live in an ever more sheltered and structured world. In recent years we have very much woken up to the fact that exposure to green spaces and fresh air is essential for a healthy body and mind. There is evidence that behavioural and emotional disorders are on the rise – not surprisingly, given how much time children spend cooped up inside.[465] The term 'nature deficit disorder,'[466] coined by Richard Louv, describes the situation very well. We have got to a stage where our children are actually developing clinical symptoms due to the lack of time they spend outdoors and engaging in nature-related activities. Finding new ways to learn and play outside will perhaps not be the cure for all our problems, but raising awareness can lead to initiatives on our children's behalf and help introduce preventative measures. It can also help with learning lifelong skills and acquiring knowledge which might otherwise be irretrievably lost.

# Ask the expert: Karen Slattery, founder of Nurture in Nature outdoor playgroup in Galloway

Karen is one of those dedicated mums who live their idea of community and being in a natural environment with their kids as much as possible. They spend the summer at festivals and sleep in yurts, travel with their children to Morocco and are always ready to help out. They are part of a network of and for people where they swap and share and help each other out. The parents and preschoolers who meet once a week in the woods benefit

465 https://www.ncbi.nlm.nih.gov/pmc/articles/PMC5803568/
466 http://richardlouv.com/; see also http://www.gaiatheory.org/

from her knowledge of the natural world. She always has something up her sleeve. A nice story is read, creepy-crawly animals found and carefully looked at, and games are played. Sometimes she invites other people, like foraging experts, to join the group. But it is best to let her describe in her own words what a 'typical' day in the woods looks like.

*How can outdoor play benefit both parents and children of all ages?*

There is a growing evidence base for the health benefits of spending time outdoors for both children and adults. With an increase in exercise, fresh air, creative inspiration and exploration, it improves fine and gross motor skills, strengthens immune systems and improves mental health.

But for me, the main benefit of outdoor play is the connection it creates to the natural world around us. To stop and appreciate wildlife, explore a stream, hide amongst the roots of a tree, allows us to reconnect with nature and with each other, no matter what age you are.

*How can babies participate, and how can it be beneficial to them?*

Babies participate simply by being there. Everything a young mind learns is through sensory experience. So, feeling the wind on their skin, hearing the rain on the trees or birdsong, seeing the sun shining through the leaves at the top of a tree, hearing other children run and play – these are all important for cognitive development.

As they get a bit older, babies can explore textures through stones, pine cones, sand, and experience a variety of colours, sounds, smells and tastes from the earth. As the seasons pass, what they can explore will change, so you have introduced them to a stimulating and ever-changing learning environment. In the first three years of life, the rate at which the synapses in the brain form will depend on the richness of the sensory environment.[467] By playing outdoors with your baby from early on, you are offering them a great start in life.

*What are the main themes around which you organise your outings?*

This has changed over the years. Initially, we got funding to start up and promote the outdoor group. To encourage people to come, we had one morning in the woods each week for ten weeks, with professional storytellers, artists, musicians and forest school leaders leading the sessions. But that was over five years ago. Now the group is an informal gathering of families, and we try out different themes which change with parents' and children's interests.

At one time the group was predominantly toddlers, so we would focus on different colours for a few weeks, then counting for a few weeks, etc. Now we have newborn babies and up to six-year-olds coming regularly, so we focus instead on a nature theme. In recent sessions, we have learned about bats, winter trees, fungi and tracking. Where possible we celebrate seasonal events (e.g. the equinox or solstice) or unusual weather, so if it's windy we won't go into the woods, but we'll make and fly kites in the meadow. All these themes are underpinned by a desire to feel connected to nature and to learn about it with a sense of awe and excitement.

---

467 https://www.ncbi.nlm.nih.gov/pmc/articles/PMC3511633/

*What is the itinerary of a typical day out in the woods?*

| | |
|---|---|
| 10.00: | Meet up with other families at the entrance to the woods. |
| 10.15: | Introduce the theme or topic and head into the woods looking for signs and thinking about the theme. |
| 10.30: | arrive at a site in the woods and play a game or tell a story. |
| 11.00: | Snack/drink time. |
| 11.30: | Do an activity or exploration linked to the theme. |
| 13.00: | Think about heading off. |
| 13.30: | Start heading back to the car park. |
| 14.00: | Leave for home. |

Although children generally respond well to structure, when we play outdoors, all sessions are flexible. Plans will change due to weather, numbers, age range and children's interests. If they decide that today they want to be pirates sailing a ship on fallen trees, then fine.

Also, the site we go to is sometimes determined in advance (some are very good for bluebells, or have a fire circle), but generally the children are free to choose where we go. Although it is preferable that they agree to go to the same place, if they have to discuss and agree this decision-making process is positive – it increases the children's confidence, sense of ownership of the group, communication skills and ability to compromise (and they learn about majority voting!).

# TIP 33
## Go for Walks

*These boots are made for walking.*

The best time to start doing this is while you are still pregnant, and for as long as you possibly can. And don't just go to shopping centres or your local high street. Really get outside and "into the wild". Take time out for yourself and get away from too much technology. After the birth, as soon as you are feeling well enough, the timing of which can vary depending on the kind of delivery you had, nothing is holding you back. A walk in the garden or the park is often possible during the first couple of days after the birth of your baby. Leave your mobile phone in your pocket (or even better, in your bag or rucksack), gaze at the sky and the trees, point out colours and animals to your baby. Take your baby in your sling or baby carrier, and gradually extend your walks as you begin to feel stronger. Make sure you are prepared for the weather conditions and wear appropriate footwear. Bring some water and a healthy snack and sit down when you feel like it. For this reason, it is wise to walk along a path where you can perhaps sit on a bench. The exercise will help you shed your pregnancy weight, you'll breathe lots of fresh air, and you'll get out of the house. If you are wary of going out on your own and your partner is unable to accompany you, why not meet up with other mums for a little ramble?

As your baby grows, which is something they do remarkably well and at lightning speed, and they have learnt to sit up for longer periods of time by themselves, consider getting an outdoors baby carrier.[468] Unlike the wraps and carriers mentioned in Tip 12, these are a lot sturdier and look like a proper backpacker's kit. Apart from keeping your baby safe and cosy, they also have lots of pockets to sneak in snacks and water, and perhaps hats and sunglasses or waterproof gear, should weather conditions change. The soft padding and actual baby seat are fitted into a framework of bars which comes with a foldable leg to enable you to place the rucksack on the floor and prevent it from falling over. To find out more about walking paths in your area, have a peek at the list in the directory.

# TIP 34
## Spend Time Out in the Sunshine

*Healthy smiles!*

If you are worried about too much exposure to UV rays, remember that being outside in green spaces can improve your self-esteem and reduce tension, anger and depression.[469]

Spending a little time unprotected out in the sunshine is necessary for the body to produce Vitamin D, which enables the bones to absorb enough calcium. A 2010 study at the University of Chicago and the Loyola University School of Nursing looked more closely at this, the role this particular vitamin plays in the prevention and treatment of many chronic illnesses, and its general health benefits.[470]

---

468 https://www.deutergb.co.uk/
469 https://www.ncbi.nlm.nih.gov/pmc/articles/PMC2908269/
470https://www.ncbi.nlm.nih.gov/pmc/articles/PMC2908269/

To learn more about this particular vitamin, go back to Tip 21.

It is therefore worthwhile to rethink your choice of sunscreen as well. Using appropriate sunscreen is one of the most important steps we can take to protect our skin from potentially harmful UV rays.[471] Your product of choice should preferably be free from any ingredients which can affect our health and irreparably damage marine and other aquatic life.

Conventional sunscreens contain chemicals such as Padimate O and para-aminobenzoic acid (PABA) as well as nitrosamine-forming agents, for instance diethanolamine (DEA).[472] These form free radicals and react with sunlight, which in turn increases the risk of skin cancer.[473] Oxybenzone[474] is another ingredient of regular chemical sunscreens you can buy off the shelves. It is an endocrine disruptor and allergen, and a cause of coral bleaching and coral death.[475] Inorganic filters like titanium oxide and zinc oxide in mineral sunscreens have much lower toxicity in comparison.[476]

---

471 https://www.ncbi.nlm.nih.gov/pmc/articles/PMC3709783/

472 https://www.ewg.org/sunscreen/report/the-trouble-with-sunscreen-chemicals/

473 Learn more about natural sunscreens at https://littlegreenfootpath.com/2019/06/29/top-natural-sunscreen-brands-and-home-made-diy-sunscreen/
You may even want to try making your own sunscreen: https://pronounceskincare.com/diy-sunscreen-easy-make-need-recipe/

474 https://www.goddessgarden.com/blog/what-is-oxybenzone-and-why-is-it-in-sunscreen/

475 https://www.nytimes.com/2018/05/03/travel/hawaii-sunscreen-ban.html

476 https://www.nytimes.com/2018/05/03/travel/hawaii-sunscreen-ban.html

Remnants of sunscreens and the chemicals contained in them can reach vulnerable organisms when washed off while sea bathing or swimming in lakes and rivers, and the resulting chemical reaction can damage microscopic algae that are at the bottom of the food chain, but for this very reason are all the more essential.[477] What harms these tiny creatures is ultimately damaging to us and our entire ecosystem. There is also some uncertainty about the detrimental effects of nanoparticles on our health.[478]

Hence, a mineral or natural sunscreen is a better choice than a chemical sunblock. You can even make your own mineral sunscreen, free from nanoparticles, by following simple recipes.[479] Go back to Tip 16 to learn which brands of sunscreen are suitable for your baby.

# TIP 35
## Make Some Time for a 'Green Hour'

*The soothing colour of hope.*

The time for your 'green hour' will vary according to the time of year, of course, and either you'll be wrapped up warmly or you'll be looking for some shelter in the shade.

---

477 https://cdhc.noaa.gov/_docs/Site%20Bulletin_Sunscreen_final.pdf

478 https://www.ewg.org/sunscreen/report/nanoparticles-in-sunscreen/; https://www.sciencedirect.com/science/article/pii/S1878535217300990

479 https://pronounceskincare.com/diy-sunscreen-easy-make-need-recipe/

## *Late spring and summer*

In the summer, you can lie on a blanket in the garden. I let my little one touch the grass with her tiny feet while holding her when she was only about four months old. You can also see what you can discover yourself, like a dainty ladybird climbing up a long blade of grass, or small flowers you've never seen before after you've left your lawn uncut for a week or two.

Look at the clouds. Give your baby some nappy-free time. Just put a towel underneath to catch any accidents, stay in the shade when it gets hot and sunny, and use big muslins to cover the pram or blanket on which your baby lies. I found those activity centres which come as a play mat and two poles that cross above like a dome very useful in this respect. Let your baby feel, smell, listen and watch just by themselves, and eventually taste (much more than you would probably them want to). Integrate this into your day whenever you can, but don't pressurise yourself to do it. This special hour can also include different activities such as walking, sitting and feeding (obviously), and playing at a time of day that can vary and suits you best. You can integrate it into your daily routine even if you just have a cup of tea while feeding your baby in the morning in summer, or take them for a stroll to observe the clouds. It is meant to be beneficial for you, too. It also makes sense to bring some natural insect repellent such as lavender oil to protect yourself and your baby against bites from insects such as midges or mosquitoes.[480]

---

480 https://www.healthline.com/health/kinds-of-natural-mosquito-repellant#lemon-eucalyptusoil

## *Autumn, winter and early spring*

In the autumn, carry your baby in your baby carrier or use your pram on walking paths in the woods. Look at the leaves changing colour; perhaps collect a few. Wrap your baby up in a warm onesie and enjoy the cooler air. Try and go with the seasons; there is always something different and new to discover. Invest in a foot muff for the winter and extra blankets. If it is not pouring down with rain or freezing, a little bit of exercise in the fresh air before you head back home to sit in front of the fire with a cup of tea is a lovely activity.

# TIP 36
## Create a Sitting Spot in the Garden

*A natural nursery.*

When you start to consider what space you have available for this, it should, of course, be safe enough for a baby. It won't have to be a permanent feature, either. It should include appropriate shelter from wind and sunlight, such as trees, garden walls or windbreaks. This is especially important for babies under six months old. It could be a spot from which you can also observe wildlife and feel comfortable yourself. Ideally, things should be brought out with you to prevent going backwards and forwards to the house all the time. In the summer, I threw all the things I needed into a laundry basket, along with a parasol, some water to drink, blankets, a nappy, a towel for my baby for some nappy-free time, and a book and a notebook, which I used when she was asleep. Your sitting spot can also vary according to season and personal preference. Play hiding games and use it as a 'natural nursery'. Look for shadows, birds, items on the ground like leaves and pebbles, and encourage your baby to look for them. Watch what goes into that little mouth, though, by the time your baby starts mouthing everything. Another way to play is through imitation. Mimic behaviour like animal sounds, or pretend a leaf is a bird. Try less structured activities, with very few tools or equipment necessary. Curl up together for a nap on a picnic blanket. In the winter you can bring in items such as a pine cone after your walk outside. Look at leaves in frozen puddles, touch the snow, and see if you can spot some wildlife, such as robins or squirrels or sometimes even a fox. There is still a possibility to nip out and enjoy the stillness. All of this will change before you know it and there will be very little sitting involved. Enjoy it while you can.

# TIP 37
## Talk to Your Baby About What You See Outside

*Interactive communication.*

Rotate your senses![481] If you think this sounds odd, it simply means using every single one of your senses to take it all in and enable you to have the full experience. Focusing on all sensory stimuli is an integral part of playful learning (see Chapter 7 for more about learning). Tell your baby about the gurgling stream, the rustling leaves, and stop to

---

481https://www.ncbi.nlm.nih.gov/pmc/articles/PMC4059790/

listen. Tell them about the warmth of the sunshine. Touch the bark of the tree. Look at the sky. Listen to birds. Smell the dampness of the earth, the moss, and of course try to taste things if it is safe to do so. In the early autumn you can forage for blackberries. Your baby's little hands will naturally move to their mouth at some point, and are part of exploring the senses. Their attention span at this stage is short, but your baby absorbs everything, and the early stages of learning begin at this age.[482] Your baby will pick up on your feelings, and the more relaxed you are, the more relaxed your baby will be (see Tip 43).

# TIP 38
## Take Your Baby Out on a Family Picnic

*Got the munchies?*

Contrary to common opinion, taking your baby out is particularly easy if you breastfeed (see Tip 3). There won't be an extra bag with bottles and other equipment – baby's packed lunch comes straight from your body. Even when out in cafes, there are ways to perfect the skill of breastfeeding in public (mainly by becoming less self-conscious about it), and to my knowledge, nobody has ever felt offended while I was feeding my daughter.[483] Lunch boxes can be filled up with home-made wraps and pasta and pesto. These are relatively easy to prepare. And it's a perfect opportunity for a family outing. Prepare healthy

---

482 Go back to the passage on executive function in Chapter 7.
483 For a discussion on why this should be considered perfectly normal and not a problem at all, go back to Chapter 1.

organic food instead of pre-packaged meals, sugary drinks and processed food. Nothing is wrong with a granola bar from time to time, but it should be a treat and not seen as a healthy option.[484] Don't bring disposable cutlery, cups and plates, even if they are biodegradable, such as cornstarch plates. Go for a stainless-steel lunch box instead,[485] and use reusable coffee mugs and bottles.

# TIP 39
## Visit Zoos, Wildlife Parks or Aquariums

*The great menagerie 2.0.*

Conditions for animals in captivity have improved tremendously over the past two generations or so. Very often this is the only chance and the last resort to save endangered species or provide facilities to rescue marine wildlife like abandoned seal pups. Such places are also important hubs of research and education, especially for children, and these days a lot of them make an effort to be interactive and great fun. These places can be an excellent resource to spark an interest in the natural world from very early on. It is a worthwhile thing to do even when your baby is still very young, and can turn out to be another enjoyable

---

484 It is possibly healthier than a Mars bar but it is still full of sugar, most brands use palm oil and they have a very high calorific content.

485 Consider replacing your old plastic lunch boxes (which are very often not made to last) with stainless-steel boxes like the Elephant Box. You can purchase these through the website https://www. anythingbutplastic.co.uk, and some of the funds go towards elephant rescue.

family outing. Babies are very receptive to colours and sounds, so this is the right time to start to show them their first glimpse of native and non-native wildlife.

# TIP 40

## Keep Pets (Dogs, Cats or Smaller Animals), or Meet Up with Friends Who Have Them

*The magic woof.*

Having pets is a great thing, no doubt. And yet there can be different reasons why you may decide against having one, or at least for the time being, such as travel plans and various other commitments which make it difficult to care for your pet in the way they need and deserve. My daughter's love for dogs became apparent by the time she was about a year old. As soon as she could run and felt secure on her own two feet, she would just take off and forget all about me, wanting to stroke any four-legged furry creature within sight. You won't have this problem with young babies, but I learnt very quickly to ask the dog's owner first and make sure my daughter understood the importance of this from very early on.

That said, our fellow creatures can significantly enrich our lives and be wonderful companions. You can do a lot for your family as well as the environment by cooking pet food from scratch instead of piling up tins and aluminium foil, or sourcing from green retailers instead.[486] Be careful with cat litter, however, as the recommendation

---

486 https://www.green-petfood.com/

is not to handle soiled litter while you are pregnant or breastfeeding.[487]

# TIP 41
## Create a Child-Friendly Wildlife Garden

*Creepy-crawly haven (or heaven).*

It is preferable to think about this at an early stage, perhaps even while you're still pregnant. It's not much of a problem before your baby develops an interest in investigating the unknown and begins to find anything dangerous irresistible. There are ways to alter your wetland installation or make it toddler-proof. Miniature wetlands are a safer alternative to a full-size pond, or build a little fountain from pebbles. You'll probably find there isn't much time for these sorts of things, but maybe it would be helpful to think of it as an ongoing project. Ask your husband/partner or other family members and friends for help, leave a bit of your lawn uncut in the corner of your garden, set up a compost heap and a wild spot, which can consist of a pile of small branches and twigs which will be an excellent habitat for woodlice. Maybe even build a small bug hotel. The RSPB website[488] has some excellent resources for this. Build a cairn for toads, which is nothing more than an upturned terracotta flowerpot and some stones, or leave so-called hedgehog highways in your fences. Tarmacking the whole of your front garden and

---

487 https://www.pregnancybirthbaby.org.au/things-to-avoid-during-pregnancy

488 https://www.rspb.org.uk/get-involved/activities/give-nature-a-home-in-your-garden/garden-activities/build-a-bug-hotel/

keeping everything else clipped and growing two pots of gardenia is certainly not an alternative.

One of the best things for our bee and butterfly populations is to keep things a little bit 'untidy'. Therefore, it isn't very time-consuming either and certainly isn't anything to get too stressed about. This time can also be used to research what works best for you and what is suitable in your garden; for example, finding out about native plants which attract native wildlife, as these of course always go together. If you happen to have an old garden, it is worthwhile to see what comes up in spring and summer and observe the life cycle of your borders before you dig them up. After that, you can think about planting some bulbs to complete or add to the variety. Maybe also think about which of them are poisonous, as this will be an issue as your baby grows older and more independent. I was shocked to see an enormous flowering monkshood in my garden which was quite precariously within my daughter's reach.

# TIP 42
## Go to the Beach

*Sand between our toes.*

The beach has its hazards, but it is a lovely way to spend some time outdoors and make a little jaunt of it, holiday feeling included. Mostly, it becomes more of an issue when your baby can crawl or walk, as they can get too close to the waves or rocky promontories before you know it.

Exposure to the sun and wind is always an issue by the sea, however, so go well prepared. Take a windbreak, mats and lots of lightweight blankets. Think also of the benefits of walking on your own bare feet.[489] Look at what's around you. Collect some shells as keepsakes[490] for your baby to cherish when they are older, or as part of your sensory bag (see Tip 28). You can also see a beach trip as an opportunity to do something for your health and fitness; albeit that these walks are limited time wise initially. In warm weather, white cotton clothes and a floppy hat are essential. The beach offers your baby a great introduction to a different environment; the breeze, salty air and negative ions included.[491] Iodine in the air is also beneficial for your health.[492] If you live far from the sea, perhaps think about spending some time at the seaside at the weekend or during your next holiday (see Tip 46).

Walks on the beach in the winter can be a satisfying activity, too. If your baby is still young, an Aran sweater[493] might even fit on top of the sling with your baby in it as you front-carry. Otherwise, get a coat extender[494] or make your own by sewing either side of a zip onto a piece of fabric to zip into your coat[495] to make it fit over your baby in their carrier or sling. I would go out in my wellies with

---

489 http://www.thebarefootbook.com/

490 Collecting specimens is fine in the vast majority of wild places, but occasionally it is illegal: https://www.theguardian.com/uk/2007/apr/06/books.booksnews

491 https://www.telegraph.co.uk/lifestyle/wellbeing/diet/3355947/Be-beside-the-seaside.html

492 https://www.liverdoctor.com/the-sea-air-is-good-for-your-thyroid/

493 https://www.aransweatermarket.com/

494 https://zipusin.co.uk/

495 Look here for some DIY ideas: https://www.pinterest.co.uk/pin/192036371591311088/; https://dineandtwine.wordpress.com/2014/09/23/baby-belly-maternitybabywearing-jacket-extension-panel/

my daughter in a padded onesie in the Ergobaby and use my big coat (the one I bought two sizes above my usual size when I was pregnant). It worked perfectly on a lovely, sunny day in January.

# TIP 43
## Calm Your Baby Through Nature[496]

*Hush, little baby...*

Being calm yourself is very likely to have a positive effect on your baby. If it gets all too much in the house: *get out!* It really helps. Balance your screen time with time outside as much as possible. Screen time does not just mean time spent working on the computer. It also includes the time we spend texting, being busy on social media, browsing the internet, gaming, generally using our mobile phones or tablets, or watching TV.

Take some time without any distractions and feel how time slows down. Breathe carefully and consciously. Sit on a swing with your baby in their carrier when they are still very young. When they are older, look out for a padded carrier in which they can sit securely. Sing a song out in the woods or when you are walking across a field. And as your baby calms down, let them go to sleep in their carrier or pushchair, which allows you to think about a thing or two other than household chores. It works wonders, I find.

---

496 https://www.naturalchild.org/guest/claire_niala.html

# TIP 44
## Join a Nurture in Nature Group

*Nature trail hunters!*

As your baby grows older and is interacting ever more with their surroundings, finding playmates is one of the most important things you can do for them. This also includes older children. So what better setting could there be than a walk in the woods while meeting other people for outside play? Nurture in Nature groups are a lovely opportunity to meet like-minded people, get some gentle exercise in the fresh air and have your baby spend some time in the company of other children, which is of great social and educational benefit. From very early on, gentle movement and exposure to laughter and happiness matter a great deal – as they do in later years. Some of these forest schools can be a little more structured as your child grows older, but the set-up can be such as to enable you to drift in and out of it and perhaps not attend every week if you can't manage to do so. Let it be partly structured and partly unstructured, and explore![497] Parents have a chance to swap stories, have a picnic and become part of the local community.

Libraries or community centres are often good hubs to find out about activities such as this. There is still such a thing as the local noticeboard. Joining (or founding) a Facebook group can also be worthwhile. To find out how a forest school works, go back to the interview with Karen Slattery at the start of this chapter.

---

497 A brilliant resource for this is https://www.childrenandnature.org

# TIP 45
## Grow Houseplants

*Indoor jungle!*

The idea that houseplants can act as air purifiers has been haunting the internet for a long time. Most of this stems from a famous NASA report[498] which was published back in 1989. The scientists involved in the project suggested – on the basis of their laboratory data – that there are some health benefits to growing indoor plants.

There is now a plethora of posts presenting top-ten or top-twenty lists of specific plants that supposedly filter all the toxins from your indoor air.[499] The downside to these lists is mainly the lack of thorough research into how this is supposed to work effectively in the setting of a private home. Most of the findings considering the efficiency of houseplants as air purifiers are, it seems, down to laboratory conditions which are difficult to reproduce in our homes.[500]

Nonetheless, most houseplants are relatively easy to grow and can help to make your house look greener and more comfortable. Here is a short list of common houseplants and their alleged benefits:

---

498 https://ntrs.nasa.gov/archive/nasa/casi.ntrs.nasa.gov/19930073077. pdf

499 https://www.theguardian.com/lifeandstyle/2004/oct/23/shopping. homes1

500 http://www.gardenmyths.com/garden-myth-born-plants-dont-purify-air/

ALOE VERA: These marvellous plants release oxygen just as plants commonly do, but also filter out remnants of benzene, a component of detergents and plastics, as well as formaldehyde in varnishes and laminate floorings[501]. There are varieties apart from the most common one, which is *Aloe aristata*. There is the hedgehog aloe (*Aloe humilis*), the partridge breast (*Aloe variegata*, named after the patterning of its leaves), and the tree aloe (*Aloe arborescens*). They evolved in arid conditions and therefore mainly need sunshine, fresh air (open the windows, and allow them some time outdoors in summer!) and water in the growing season, and a cool and dry resting period, i.e. winter dormancy.

ENGLISH OR COMMON IVY: *Hedera helix* is supposed to remove seventy-eight per cent of airborne mould in just twelve hours[502]. This plant thrives in unheated rooms but suffers in the hot, dry air of centrally heated rooms.

PEACE LILY: *Spathiphyllum wallisii* is thought to improve your indoor air by absorbing mould spores, as it uses them as food and circulates them through its leaves to its roots[503]. These plants are a bit more demanding but still do well if kept out of direct sunlight and in a reasonably warm room in winter.

SPIDER PLANT: This humble little plant, *Chlorophytum comosum variegatum* with its web-like or spider-legged

---

501 https://blog.smarttouchenergy.com/houseplants-air-filters
502 https://learn.allergyandair.com/english-ivy-and-mold/
503 https://myecohub.com/product/peace-lily/

leaves, removes up to ninety per cent of toxins and is helpful for those suffering from dust allergies[504]. These foliage plants are not fussy and will grow in hot or cool rooms, on sunny windowsills or in shady corners, and don't mind dry air.

The main benefits of an indoor garden are not due to the plants themselves but mainly to the soil in the flowerpots. Think about what we bring into our homes, such as hand sanitisers, detergents, sprays etc. to get rid of all the 'dirt' and 'germs' and everything we have been taught to be afraid of (the emphasis is on *taught*). Luckily, we are becoming increasingly aware that these chemicals are far more harmful than a few specks of dirt (something to think about even more when you have young children, especially babies and/or toddlers).[505] Benign bacteria we inhale or ingest with a bit of soil while outside can also be beneficial for our capacity to learn, as some research by the American Society for Microbiology suggests.[506]

So, try and bring a bit of greenery indoors – but remember, you should still spend some time outside, preferably each day, other than walking from the car into a building and back!

---

504 https://www.diyncrafts.com/4457/home/top-10-nasa-approved-houseplants-improving-indoor-air-quality

505 https://www.nwf.org/~/media/PDFs/Be%20Out%20There/Dirt_Report_2012.ashx

506 https://www.eurekalert.org/pub_releases/2010-05/asfm-cbm052010.php (Also see Tip 22.)

# TIP 46
## Go on a Holiday with Lots of Time Outdoors

*Family ramblers...*

Unlike package holidays, individually planned ones leave a lot of time for spontaneity. If you have a caravan or motorhome, you can easily include the outdoor factor. The confined space in a caravan can get you in a bit of a pickle as it leaves little opportunity for baby to crawl about or sit safely, not to mention the stage when they start opening drawers at every opportunity, squashing their tiny fingers. So, it is best to childproof your caravan just as you did your home. You might want to wait before using a tent, but once again it's up to you. It is worth thinking about not being too far from amenities, should they be required. Gentler activities may be the thing to go for to begin with, such as gentle walks. It is quite possible to carry a very young baby in a sling while exploring the rock pools of Easdale Island near Oban in the west of Scotland, as I have found myself.

At this stage, there is the freedom to book your holiday without heeding the big school holidays, unless you have older children already. By opting for a holiday in the UK or Europe, you can also reduce your carbon footprint. If you want to visit the Continent, consider taking the ferry instead of flying.[507]

507 A lot of them have stopped operating altogether, but do check other possibilities than the Dover-to-Calais route. Some of them are competitively priced and a great alternative to the often stressful hustle and bustle of an airport. And think of the reduced carbon footprint!

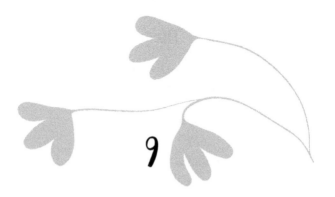

# 9

# Mindfulness

*Model kindness and children learn kindness. Model distance and they learn distance. There's time for limits and boundaries, but not in infancy. If you model empathy, responsiveness, trust, kindness, and compassion, there's a good chance that's what you'll get when you're elderly and dependent on him.*

La Leche League, *Sweet Sleep*[508]

## TIP 47
### Keep it Simple

*I did it my way...*

I will now share with you a golden rule: always regard other people and their stories with a critical eye. Don't

---

508 J. E. Swain et al., 'Toward a neuroscience of interactive parent-infant dyad empathy' in *Behavioral and Brain Sciences* 2013, 36 (4): 438–9.

take everything at face value. It is a bit like getting rid of surplus stuff: declutter your mind from advice and ideas that isn't useful for your situation or does not sit well with you personally. That includes things you have read in this book that you feel are not relevant to or right for you.

The reason is this: *you* need to listen to *your* child, and to *yourself*. That is a skill we have lost these days because we are (seemingly) so short of time and stressed and only waiting for the next notification from some app or other to tell us what to do. Trusting our instincts is very much a lost art. It's basically about not having a plan and gently responding to your child's needs, which are pretty basic, to be frank, yet we seem to think we need to be armed to our teeth and ready for it – whatever 'it' might be. The fact is that most of the time you won't know what's coming and nothing will prepare you for it. It can be of some help once you realise that you have already got what your child needs the most, which is yourself (and yes, that is just the way you are). A baby's needs are also their wants, which is why that tiny human being doesn't have ulterior motives and isn't trying to trick you into anything – that is most likely to come much later. Child psychologists reckon that babies experience themselves as an extension of their closest caregiver. They see themselves as one with them and their surroundings[509] – perhaps this sounds a bit like Buddhist nirvana, but I think there is a lot to learn by just watching babies. We are bound to find ourselves becoming distracted, stressed or annoyed when we are feeling so terribly exhausted. We might say things we'll regret later on,

---

509 http://uk.sagepub.com/sites/default/files/upm-binaries/13948_
    Roberts.pdf

only to realise that this tiny bundle of ever-abundant energy is the best thing that ever happened to us. So, we should lie down, hold our babies and look up at the sky, the trees, a pond – you get the picture. Sometimes that is all we need.

You can also achieve a lot in a few snippets of time, and for this, of course, some routine is helpful. Early on, I found it beneficial to lay out everything I was going to wear in the morning, get up while my daughter was still asleep and be fully dressed, teeth brushed and hair combed etc., before she was awake. It didn't always work as sometimes she was awake already or even crying while I tried to make my hair-brushing engaging for her. I felt a lot better when I was ready to meet the day, dressed and washed and hair combed instead of lounging about in my nightdress. It was also easier to look after my baby and everything else that needed my attention. This practice slowly evolved by the time she was about six to eight weeks old, as before that I stayed in bed much longer. After I had healed and felt ready to meet the world again, I tried to put some of these rhythms in place for us. I prefer to call them that instead of 'routine' or 'schedule' as I feel that I was trying to initiate things while reacting to my daughter's cues at the same time.

All of this is more important than trying to distract your baby with heaps of toys. Especially in the early days, they need very little equipment to be entertained. A lot of things you might not even have thought of as play can easily be converted into a game, even cleaning jobs around the house. I always told my daughter that she was a great help simply by watching me quietly while being carried in a sling or baby carrier on my back. I regularly explained to her what I was doing and thereby interacted with her. Later on, I made folding up washing into a game. I gave her half of it to play with, while I folded the other half up and then stored it away. When I continued with the rest, she was quite happy with another toy or the laundry basket itself. Use the simplest items for your baby to hold and feel in order to develop a very tangible sense of the world that surrounds him. As your baby gets older, a duvet or rug can be a boat at sea, with soft toys and yourselves as the passengers.

Use your hands and a torch to stage a shadow play. Make time without TV or any other gadgets. I could repeat myself and talk about how our 'modern' way of life causes our communities to disintegrate and how increasingly fragmented they have become. But most of the time, we have to deal with whatever is presenting itself to us. Prioritise, minimise and focus (and refocus). Before long, it will change again. Let your baby teach and inspire you. All this talk about being in the moment – babies and children are certainly experts at this, so perhaps don't try to drive it out of them right from the start. Continue to keep it simple!

# TIP 48
## Take Care of Your Mental Health and Well-Being

*Light in the dark recesses of the mind.*

I would like to suggest a little meditation practice. Cast your mind back to the days when you were attending antenatal classes. Your nest-building instinct may have been in full swing. Perhaps you felt you were barely able to move because of your enormous belly. And then they told you about this thing called postnatal depression, or PND for short.[510]

Just melting into motherhood seemed like an easy thing to do by all accounts, although for a lot of us this is not likely to be the case. As pressures are mounting to get our lives back as soon as possible, while being scrutinised for our mothering abilities, even the most confident of us may crack at some point.[511]

But here is the good news: you can do something about it, and there is support in place.[512] Postnatal depression is a severe condition, as anyone who has suffered from it will be able to tell you. While it may occur due to hormonal reasons, it can also be sparked by isolation, lack of support and exhaustion. It seems inevitable that we face some difficulties when adjusting to the changes in our bodies and minds after giving birth. We may feel that our old life is irrevocably lost. How can we regain our former selves? How can we cope? There are so many reasons why things can be difficult, such as a problematic relationship or an unplanned pregnancy. Sometimes the baby suffers from health issues, or other things happen. Maybe another family member also needs your care.

Pregnancy, and its far-longer-lasting outcome – parenthood, is a rite of passage[513] and you indeed have

---

510 http://www.uppitysciencechick.com/postpartum-depression.html

511 S. Maushart, *The Mask of Motherhood: How Becoming a Mother Changes Our Lives and How We Never Talk About It* (2000), and https://herviewfromhome.com/new-mom-takes-her-own-life-after-silent-battle-with-postpartum-depression-why-all-of-us-must-share-her-friends-plea/

512 http://www.pandasfoundation.org.uk/

513 Read more about this from my very personal point of view at https://littlegreenfootpath.com/2018/03/

become a new person. It is about letting go, and it can perhaps even be called a spiritual experience. It is also time to remind yourself that nothing stays the same, and the gift of a child and parenthood is something to be embraced. This also includes perhaps not giving up things but replacing them with something new, hitherto unknown and different. Grant yourself the time it takes to come to terms with the changes in your life. Be patient initially; enjoy the natural break until you're fully recovered or feeling well enough to slowly take up some of your jobs again. And never be afraid to ask for help, although very often this is foisted upon you. Likewise, don't be afraid to refuse it. A lot of the mood swings you are experiencing at this stage are due to hormonal changes which are beyond your control – or so we assume. Allow yourself that weakness and remember that keeping it simple or gentle also includes yourself. Even consider counselling if needs must. Even though one shouldn't measure oneself against others all the time, remind yourself of the circumstances you're in and adjust accordingly. If any of this applies to you, please don't hesitate to seek help.

# TIP 49
## Give Your Baby the Continuum Concept[514]

*An unbroken biological chain.*

In the 1970s, a young woman called Jean Liedloff spent some years living with the Ye'kuana (also commonly referred to as Makiritare) in the Venezuelan jungle. This led to a radical

514 http://www.continuum-concept.org/

change in her preconceptions and beliefs about how we should live and bring up our children, and what human nature is. The tribe still lives in the tropical rainforest zone in parts of southern Venezuela and a small section of northern Brazil. Today, there are about 2,200 Ye'kuana living in 35 villages which are organised in a tribal-Amazonian system, whose prime asset is an egalitarian social structure.[515] In factual terms, it means that the village headman does not enforce rules by coercive power and decision-making processes are achieved by consensus.[516]

The core of Liedloff's theory is that the innate expectations with which an infant of our species is born are, in an evolutionary sense, those of a mammalian predator. Theoretically speaking, this means we are all part of an evolutionary continuum written into our DNA. It makes us who we are. It is the blueprint with which we are born and by which we are made to function in our ecological niche.

Mammals cannot survive without their mothers. Other species, such as fish, amphibians and reptiles usually do (there are a few exceptions[517]), birds less so. Mammalian

---

515 As Europeans, North Americans, Australians of European descent and most Asian nations and also African nations we will probably find that our terminology falls short of describing their and other tribespeople's way of life correctly. Even the word "egalitarian", which is rooted in European political philosophy, is only an approximation: https://plato.stanford.edu/entries/egalitarianism/

516 Read more about the tribe's fight for cultural survival and self-determination: https://www.culturalsurvival.org/publications/cultural-survival-quarterly/yekuana-southern-venezuela

517 https://daily.jstor.org/how-non-mammals-nurse-their-young/; https://www.nationalgeographic.com/animals/2018/11/spiders-nurse-young-with-milk-lactation-arachnids/

young are the ones that are the most dependent on their mothers for food, warmth and shelter.[518] A lot of mammals, including humans, are born in a so-called altricial state, which means they are completely helpless for quite some time after birth needing extensive care, although there are some exceptions such as cetaceans who will need to be able to swim postpartum or artiodactyls (notably wildebeest or giraffes) who will need to able to walk.[519] When your baby cries they communicate their fear of abandonment, which simply means: I am afraid I am going to die. That is why babies are uncomfortable when being left in a dark room by themselves. It feels instinctively unnatural to them to be parted from us, or to be put down or rocked in a pram instead of feeling the sway of our body moving around. They won't try and trick you or test their boundaries at this stage – that will all come later. For now, their instinct is to want to be carried, to feel your heartbeat, and your physical closeness. That is how they feel safe and how they are assured that you are there to look after them. It may all seem unrealistic these days, but that is where, according to Liedfloff's theory, the continuum has been broken. So, when we say, we don't have the time to look after them, something is amiss. We are acting against our natural instinct and creating the root cause of our society's major problems. Of course, our culture is ever so influential in shaping us as an individual and as part of the group or nation in which we live, but our biology is, put simply, the hardwiring which makes us work. As Liedloff observed, and formulated as the basis of her theory, the breaking of this continuum will

---

518 https://animaldiversity.org/accounts/Mammalia/
519 https://animaldiversity.org/accounts/Mammalia/;

lead to agony and constant strife to make up for this lack of nurturing and reassurance in the earliest days of infancy. That is, in short, the Continuum Concept.

Reading her book while I was pregnant made me realise how we have deprived ourselves of our very basic needs, which certainly aren't toys and money. It gets worse when you understand, as Liedloff convincingly argues, how this kind of deprivation leads to antisocial behaviour and addiction while never actually being able to attain our goal, which is ultimately not a goal but a state of being which is natural to our species. We identify it as 'joy' and 'happiness'. Part of this is giving your baby the essential in-arms stage for the first six months of their life, during which we should almost always carry our infants. Just stop for a minute and think of our closest biological relatives, the great apes, and how they treat their young. If you wonder how on earth you can ever manage the household without placing your baby in a bouncy chair in front of the TV, turn back to the section on baby carriers (Tip 12).

Soothe your baby and help them along on their steep learning curve to independence and self-reliance. None of this will be brought on by forceful separation, early weaning, formula feeding, sleep training, crying it out, dummies, bouncers, baby monitors, electric rockers or mountains of plastic toys. Respond to their cries; it is the only way they can communicate their distress. Keep them close – it is their lifeline, their safety net, and will teach them lifelong confidence in themselves and you. Breastfeed and co-sleep. It will make life easier, better and most of all happier for your child, yourself and your partner, and very likely for everyone else around you and, ultimately, human society.

# TIP 50
## Make Room for Togetherness, Imagination, Stillness and Love

*The life of the mind.*

Spend lots of time with your baby. Let them touch your face or try to bite your nose or chin, or play with your hands instead of using plastic toys. Your own well-being is essential for your baby to grow and develop healthily (see Tip 47). The authors of La Leche League's book *Sweet Sleep* refer to it as 'Magnetic Mothering', whereby two halves of one piece are allowed to snap together. Attachment in this sense means to stick together in a relationship, which for infants means touch and holding. It gradually evolves into attunement, a 'read-your-mind' relationship, which also means that one interacts when both are feeling social and stops when it is getting too much.[520]

To me, it is all about sharing and giving your baby the experience of being loved and wanted. Not a single toy, however expensive or exclusive, can replace this as your baby wants to share their life with *you* and not be made to feel that they have taken away some freedom from you. Ask yourself about the importance of these things at this stage. In this sense, it has a lot to do with going green, as we need very little. What we do need is help and support – not only from health professionals and officials, but more so from family and friends. These days, families often live some distance apart, which doesn't necessarily mean that

---

520 Read more in La Leche League, *Sweet Sleep* (2014), Chapter 3, loc. 31ff.

they aren't close emotionally. Always remind yourself that this is only going to be a very short time which offers magnificent rewards. It means juggling jobs around the house, playing with your baby, taking them to different places and at the same time being on top of what you deem necessary or 'can't-do-without'. Maybe think about writing down a list of the things you seem to have lost, such as going out and uninterrupted sleep, and those you have gained, even just other people admiring your baby. Think about the fact that this little person loves you best in the whole world. Or that you have the opportunity to make new friends, people you might never have met otherwise. Most of the time it's not all about swapping stories of our experiences of childcare, often dismissed as 'mummy talk'. You'll be surprised what's possible. You might even discover a new interest.

While it is true that very young children thrive on daily rhythms and weekly activities they recognise, it is all part of making them feel that you are reliable. They will feel safe and secure. But there will be disturbances at times, let's be realistic. It is impossible to have the exact same routine every single day, and as your baby grows into a toddler, whatever routine you have established will naturally evolve into the next stage. It can often feel as though you are struggling through it, but that is fine too as long as you find ways to adapt and respond to the changes you are observing in your child. And these things cannot be rushed. After a bit of a muddle, life usually resumes a calmer pace. When my daughter was about eighteen months old, I had to make a lot of changes as she became ever more independent and I was in awe of how capable she already was. I found the books by Simone Davies and

Julia Palmarola on implementing the Montessori Method at home very helpful in this respect.[521]

By the time my baby was six months old, everything changed again; not to mention when she started crawling at about eight to nine months and our house became the most dangerous place on the planet – or so I thought sometimes. It is, therefore, a process of continually adapting and readapting to circumstances and new patterns as your baby learns and discovers the world at lightning speed – a lot quicker, by the way, than you do. By the time your baby is about ten to eleven months old, they will have undergone a complete metamorphosis, from a tiny bundle who was happily asleep in your sling into a speed-crawling, grab-anything-that-is-potentially-dangerous, wriggly, giggly whirlwind. You probably won't believe that your tiny baby is ever going to turn into one of those strong, scary giants you have hitherto observed from a safe enough distance. I mean those who go into a tantrum at Tesco's and know the effectiveness of throwing themselves on the floor or arching their backs when you pick them up, or who decide to refuse to have their bath: toddlers. Just take a deeeeep breath and move on! Share, connect and enjoy the freedom of being!

---

521 There is a whole plethora of different books and websites you can peruse on this topic. Those by S. Davies and J. Palmarola (see Recommended Reading) are just two very recent ones on the subject which I happened to get my hands on and they were both very good. So, if you are ready to look ahead, read and read more.

# Recommended Reading

**Lisa Barnes,** *Cooking for Baby: Wholesome, Homemade, Delicious Foods for 6 to 18 Months* (2015).

**Emery & Durga Bernhard,** *A Ride on Mother's Back: A Day of Baby Carrying Around the World* (1996).

**Kate Blincoe,** *The No-Nonsense Guide to Green Parenting: How to Raise Your Child, Help Save the Planet and Not Go Mad* (2016).

**Maria Blois,** *Babywearing: The Benefits and Beauty of This Ancient Tradition* (2005).

**Amy Brown,** *Breastfeeding Uncovered: Who Really Decides How We Feed Our Babies?* (2016).

**Melissa Corkhill,** *Green Parenting: The Best for You, Your Children and the Environment* (2006).

**Simone Davies,** *The Montessori Toddler: A Parent's Guide to Raising a Curious and Responsible Human Being* (2019).

**Pam England,** *Ancient Map for Modern Birth: Preparation, Passage, and Personal Growth during your Childbearing Years* (2017).

**Kate Evans,** *The Food of Love: Your Formula for Successful Breastfeeding* (2009).

**Lynda Fassa,** *Green Babies, Sage Moms: The Ultimate Guide to Raising Your Organic Baby* (2008).

**Cordelia Fine,** *Delusions of Gender: The Real Science Behind Sex Differences* (2010).

**Ina May Gaskin,** *Ina May's Guide to Childbirth* (2008).

**Sally J. Hall,** *Eco Baby: A Guide to Green Parenting* (2008).

**Joy Hatch and Rebecca Kelley,** *The Eco-Nomical Baby Guide: Down-to-Earth Ways for Parents to Save Money and the Planet* (2010).

**Deborah Jackson,** *Three in a Bed: The Benefits of Sleeping with Your Baby* (1999).

**Sheila Kippley,** *Breastfeeding and Natural Child Spacing: The Ecology of Natural Mothering* (1974).

**Vimala McClure,** *Infant Massage: A Handbook for Loving Parents* (1982).

**James McKenna,** *Sleeping with Your Baby: A Parent's Guide to Cosleeping* (2007).

**Maria Montessori,** *Absorbent Mind* (1963).

**Michel Odent,** *Birth and Breastfeeding: Rediscovering the needs of Women during Pregnancy ad Childbirth* (2003).

**Julia Palmarola,** *Practical Guide to the Montessori Method at Home: With More Than 100 Activity Ideas from 0 to 6* (2018).

**Gabrielle Palmer,** *The Politics of Breastfeeding: When Breasts are Bad for Business* (2009).

**Elspeth and Fiona Richards,** *Playtime: Activities for Little Children That Can Make a Big Difference* (2010).

**Jenn Savedge,** *The Everything Green Baby Book: From Pregnancy to Baby's First Year – an Easy and Affordable Guide to Help You Care for Your Baby – and the Earth!* (2010).

**Diane Wiessinger, Diana West, Linda J. Smith and Teresa Pitman (La Leche League),** *Sweet Sleep: Nighttime & Naptime Strategies for the Breastfeeding Family* (2014).

# Resources Directory

## Chapter 1: Feeding and Sleeping

*Breastfeeding Information and Support*

National Childbirth Trust (NCT): https://www.nct.org.uk/

Lactation Consultants of Great Britain: https://www.lcgb.org/

The Breastfeeding Network: https://www.breastfeedingnetwork.org.uk/

Association of Breastfeeding Mothers: https://abm.me.uk/

Home-Start UK: https://www.home-start.org.uk/

La Leche League GB: https://www.laleche.org.uk/

International Baby Food Action Network: http://www.ibfan.org/

KellyMom.com: https://kellymom.com/

*Sleeping*

National Institute for Health and Care Excellence: https://www.nice.org.uk

The Lullaby Trust: https://www.lullabytrust.org.uk/

University of Notre Dame Mother-Baby Behavioral Sleep Laboratory (Dr James McKenna): https://cosleeping.nd.edu/

BASIS – Baby Sleep Info Source (University of Durham): https://www.basisonline.org.uk/

*Introducing Solids*
Baby Led Weaning: http://www.babyledweaning.com/
Soil Association: https://www.soilassociation.org
Marine Stewardship Council: https://www.msc.org
The Food Commission: http://www.foodcomm.org.uk
Compassion in World Farming: https://www.ciwf.org.uk
Fair Trade Foundation: http://www.fairtrade.org.uk/

## Chapter 2: Fashion Statements and Baby Equipment Anxiety

*Travel, Slings and Baby Carriers*
Little Possums: http://www.littlepossums.co.uk/
Wrap You in Love: https://www.wrapyouinlove.com/
Wrapping Rachel: https://wrappingrachel.com/
Royal Society for the Prevention of Accidents (RoSPA) –
    Child Car Seats: https://www.childcarseats.org.uk

*Natural Sleepy Time – Cots and Organic Mattresses*
Mokee cot: https://en.mokee.eu/cot.html
Coco-Mat: https://www.coco-mat.com/int_en/
Herdysleep: https://www.herdysleep.com/
Heal's: https://www.heals.com/natural-sleep-mohair-
    mattress.html
Latex Sense: https://www.latexsense.co.uk/
The Natural Bed Company: https://www.
    naturalbedcompany.co.uk/
Woolroom: https://www.thewoolroom.com/
The Little Green Sheep: https://www.thelittlegreensheep.
    co.uk/
Cottonsafe Natural Mattress: https://www.
    cottonsafenaturalmattress.co.uk/

*Clothing & Shoes*
Babi Pur: https://www.babipur.co.uk/
Greenfibres: https://www.greenfibres.com/
Frugi: https://www.welovefrugi.com/
Happy Little Soles: https://www.happylittlesoles.co.uk
MamaOwl: https://mamaowl.net/
Special Little Shop: https://special-little-shop.com/
Cambridge Baby: https://www.cambridgebaby.co.uk/
Fashion Revolution: https://www.fashionrevolution.org/
People Tree: https://www.peopletree.co.uk/
Toms – Shoes & Sunglasses: https://www.toms.co.uk/
Vivo Barefoot – Zero Drop & Minimalist Shoes: https://
    www.vivobarefoot.com/
Green Shoes – Handmade women's accessories, leather
    & vegan. Handmade since 1981: https://www.
    greenshoes.co.uk/

*Online Retailers and Information*
The Ethical Shop: https://ethicalshop.org/
Greencity Wholefoods: https://www.greencity.coop/
Ethical Consumer: https://www.ethicalconsumer.org/
Big Green Smile: https://www.biggreensmile.com
Ecco Verde: https://www.ecco-verde.co.uk/
Anything But Plastic: https://www.anythingbutplastic.
    co.uk/
Sinplástico: https://www.sinplastico.com/en/
Ethical Trading Initiative: https://www.ethicaltrade.org/
Save Some Green: https://www.savesomegreen.co.uk/
Natural Collection: https://www.naturalcollection.com/

*Resources, Reviews and Updates*
Child Accident Prevention Trust: https://www.capt.org.uk/

The Baby Products Association: http://www.b-p-a.org/
bpa-org/home.asp
Gimme the Good Stuff: https://gimmethegoodstuff.org/
British Standards Institution shop: https://shop.bsigroup.
com/
Global Organic Textile Standard:
https://www.global-standard.org/

## Chapter 3: Nappies

*Resources*
UK Nappy Network: http://www.uknappynetwork.org/
NappiCycle – the complete nappy recycling service:
http://nappicycle.co.uk/

*Retailers – All-in-One Nappies, Terries, Wraps and Accessories*
The Nappy Lady: https://www.thenappylady.co.uk/
Terry Nappies: https://www.terrynappies.co.uk/
Nature Babies: http://www.naturebabies.co.uk/
Easy Peasy Nappies: https://www.easypeasynappies.
co.uk/
Bambino Mio: https://www.bambinomio.com/en
Mother Ease: https://mother-ease.com/
Plush Pants Cloth Nappies: https://www.plushpants.
co.uk/
Kingdom of Fluff: https://www.kingdomfluff.co.uk/
Little Pants Nappies: http://www.littlepants.co.uk/
LittleLamb Nappies: https://littlelambnappies.com
TotsBots: https://www.totsbots.com/
Bamberoos: https://www.wonderoos.com/introducing-
bamberoos/
Mother Nature Products: https://mothernatureproducts.
co.za/

Earthlets: https://www.earthlets.com/
Twinkle Twinkle: https://www.twinkleontheweb.co.uk/

*Eco-Friendly Disposables*
Beaming Baby: https://beamingbaby.co.uk/
Rascal + Friends: https://www.rascalandfriends.co.uk/
Bambo Nature: https://bambo-nature.co.uk/
Eco by Naty: https://www.naty.com/uk/

*Swim Nappies*
Splash About: https://www.splashabout.com/
Konfidence: https://www.konfidence.co.uk/

## Chapter 4: Toiletries

Weleda: https://www.weleda.co.uk/
Lansinoh: https://lansinoh.co.uk/
Burt's Bees: https://www.burtsbees.co.uk/
Kokoso Baby Skincare: https://kokoso.co.uk/
The Konjac Sponge Co.: https://www.
    konjacspongecompany.com/
Jack n' Jill: https://www.jackandjillkids.com/
Friendly Soap: https://www.friendlysoap.co.uk/
Stop the Water While Using Me!: https://stop-the-water-
    while-using-me.com/de/
Georganics: https://georganics.com/
The Humble Co.: https://thehumble.co/
Pronounce Skincare: https://pronounceskincare.com
MooGoo Skincare: https://moogooskincare.co.uk/
Peace With The Wild – Eco Friendly & Plastic Free
    Products: https://www.peacewiththewild.co.uk/
*Also see Online Retailers section of Chapter 2 resources*

## Chapter 5: Health and Medication

PubMed – US National Library of Medicine at the
National Institutes of Health: https://www.ncbi.nlm.
nih.gov/pubmed/
World Health Organization: https://www.who.int/
Wild Nutrition Supplements: https://www.wildnutrition.
com/
Environmental Working Group: https://www.ewg.org/
National Center for Homeopathy: https://www.
homeopathycenter.org/
Vaccines – Your Best Shot at Good Health: https://www.
vaccines.gov

## Chapter 6: A Greener Home

*Cleaning*
Ecozone: https://ecozone.com/
Guppyfriend Washing Bag: http://guppyfriend.com/en/
E-Cloth: https://www.e-cloth.com/
*Also see Online Retailers section of Chapter 2 resources*

*Recycling, Energy Saving and Circular Economy*
The Freecycle Network: https://www.freecycle.org/
Nextdoor – the private social network for your
neighbourhood: https://nextdoor.co.uk/
Recycle Now – where and how to recycle: https://www.
recyclenow.com/
Love Food Hate Waste: https://www.lovefoodhatewaste.
com/
New Economy Organisers Network (NEON): https://
neweconomyorganisers.org/
Fossil Free UK: https://gofossilfree.org/uk/

Waste and Resources Action Programme (WRAP):
http://www.wrap.org.uk/
Farm Retail Association: http://www.farma.org.uk/
Waterwise: https://www.waterwise.org.uk/

## Chapter 7: Play to Learn – and Learn to Play

*Sustainable Toys*
PlanToys: http://www.plantoys.com/
Hape Wooden Toys: https://www.hape.com/uk/en
Best Years Ltd: https://www.bestyears.co.uk/en/
Lanka Kade: https://www.lankakade.co.uk/
Mushroom & Co.: https://www.naturalrubbertoys.co.uk/

*Books and Learning*
Snazal Books Wholesale: https://www.snazal.com/
NurtureStore: https://nurturestore.co.uk/
International Association of Infant Massage: http://iaim.
org.uk/
Let Toys Be Toys: http://lettoysbetoys.org.uk/

## Chapter 8: Outdoors with Baby

Richard Louv: http://richardlouv.com/
Children & Nature Network: https://www.
childrenandnature.org/
Royal Society for the Protection of Birds (RSPB): https://
www.rspb.org.uk
Gaia Theory: http://www.gaiatheory.org/
Green Petfood: https://www.green-petfood.com
Natural Resources Defense Council: https://www.nrdc.org/
Roundtable on Sustainable Palm Oil (RSPO): https://
rspo.org/

*Walking*

Walking Britain: https://www.walkingbritain.co.uk/
Ramblers: https://www.ramblers.org.uk/
Walkingworld: http://www.walkingworld.com/
The Walking Englishman: https://www.
    walkingenglishman.com/
Happy Hiker: http://www.happyhiker.co.uk/
Walkhighlands: https://www.walkhighlands.co.uk/

## Chapter 9: Mindfulness

*Attachment Parenting*

The Continuum Concept: http://www.continuum-
    concept.org/
Centre for Attachment: http://www.centreforattachment.
    com/
Center on the Developing Child (Harvard University):
    https://developingchild.harvard.edu/
Attachment Parenting International: http://www.
    attachmentparenting.org/
The Natural Child Project: https://www.naturalchild.org

*Mental Health*

House of Light – support and counselling for antenatal
    and postnatal anxiety and depression: https://
    pndsupport.co.uk/
PANDAS Foundation UK: http://www.pandasfoundation.
    org.uk/
Association for Post Natal Illness (APNI): https://apni.org/
Post Natal Illness: http://www.pni.org.uk/
Bliss – for babies born premature or sick: https://www.
    bliss.org.uk/

*General Resources*
Mama Natural: https://www.mamanatural.com/
*The Green Parent* magazine: https://thegreenparent.co.uk/
*JUNO* magazine: https://www.junomagazine.com/
*The Mother* magazine: http://www.themothermagazine.
  co.uk/

# Acknowledgements

This book could not have been written without the help of many people.

I would like to thank those who were willing to contribute their invaluable expert knowledge in the form of interviews. It would have been a different book without them. So, thank you ever so much Lauren Taylor, Karen Slatterly, Ken Goode and Jenny Walker.

My thanks also go out to the team at IndieGo for a brilliant copyedit and the hard work to bring this book on its way and making it look like, well, actually "a book".

Special thanks go out to my uncle who sponsored this book.

My husband Mark. Thank you for putting up with my writer's moods and all your loving support. My daughter Aemilia. Thank you for sleeping just before lunchtime for so many days on end to let Mummy write this book (although these naps became shorter and shorter towards the end of completing the manuscript ☺). And thank you for teaching me to be a mum.

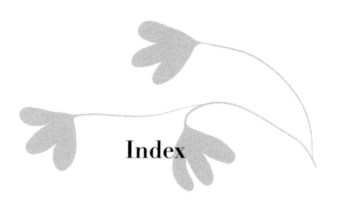

# Index

# INDEX

Lightning Source UK Ltd.
Milton Keynes UK
UKHW020809120721
387001UK00007B/884